MAKE FRIENDS WITH YOUR FLOWERING SHRUBS

JERRY BAKER

Designed and Edited by Charles Cook

Simon and Schuster   New York

We would like to thank the following individuals for providing the photos which appear in this book:

Cook—4, 9, 13, 28, 30, 67; Paris Trail—11; Roche—6, 14, 17; Wilkinson—7, 20, 21, 22, 24, 25, 27, 29, 32, 33, 39, 42, 47, 49, 51, 53, 55, 56, 57, 66.

SBN 671-21652-X Paperback
Library of Congress Catalog Card Number: 73-8220
Designed by Charles Cook
Manufactured in the United States of America

1   2   3   4   5   6   7   8   9   10

Cover photo by A. B. Morse

Contents

*"You may walk tall, Tree,
but we shrubs have more trunks."*

Flower Children

Shrubs are like playful children. Books on gardening frequently tell you to use them for background material—placing them where they can be seen but not heard. Just try this! You will soon find that practically every one of them refuses to stay put and starts clamoring for attention in no time at all.

When this happens, don't fight the feeling—smack them—hard. But tell them, as I do, that it hurts you the most so they will know you still love them. Be firm from the very beginning. Train them the way they should go and your reward will be quick and easy beauty. Well-behaved shrubs can add a lot of charm to the garden scene.

Plan before you plant, find out all about the ones you fancy most and then make your decisions wisely—that's what this book is all about.

Most shrubs are accommodating; they really want to please you, being both easy-going and easy-growing. But like teenagers, they shoot up fast. Some tend to be a bit ungainly, others flop down, and a few slip along slyly under the ground, emerging in unexpected places where they really have no business being. Some have even worked out a means of propagating themselves, called suckering, so well that they have almost entirely forgotten how to make seeds. Beware of these rascals unless you have plenty of room where they can naturalize and ramble around to their heart's content. These fellows can never be taught good manners.

Choosing the shrubs you will plant depends a lot on your own life style. If you have lots of time and a yen for adventure, you might like to grow some of the finicky things—finicky in your area, that is, for everything grows well in its native environment. But if you want lots of decorative flowers, fruit or foliage, take a tour around your town and see what the neighbors have in their yards.

Few things are more disappointing than spending a lot of time and money trying to landscape the home grounds with shrubs difficult to grow in your particular climate. Petting them along may be fun at first, but it can get very tiresome after a while, and you may start wishing you had chosen some friendly fellow less demanding of your time and attention. And this is very unfair; after all, you picked him, it wasn't the other way around.

Make things easy on yourself. If you live in a climate where crape myrtles, smoke trees, redbud or dogwood grow easily and well, why try for azaleas and rhododendrons? They may give you a hard time (and have one themselves), in a hot, dry, windy section of the country. On the other hand, if your climate is cool and moist, with the winter rest period these shrubs need, you have the ideal situation, and success is practically assured.

Gardening should always be a pleasure, never a burden. Plants that will grow and do well with a minimum of care will contribute to your peace of mind, as well as afford you great pleasure by their lovely presence.

Smoke trees demand no special growing conditions, and they put on a spectacular summer show.

Never Snub a Shrub

Invite your friends carefully. Remember they are going to be permanent residents and should be accorded all due respect, even though it may be necessary, at times, to curb their enthusiasm. For they are very important garden material, often adapting themselves to the smaller home landscape better than trees. They do not need to be replanted every year like annuals, they grow a bit taller and hardier than most perennials, and they provide at least as much decorative value as either one.

Furthermore, with a bit of care you can select varieties that will provide you with blooms all through the seasons. But shrubs often give more than this. Blossoms may be followed by berries (sometimes edible), in brilliant collors of red, orange, deep crimson, brown or black. One, the sapphireberry, is even a delightful turquoise blue.

Foliage is another important factor to consider. You should find your garden companions attractive in or out of bloom. Are their leaves large or small; a bright, glossy green, or a dull green-gray; round, heart-shaped or many fingered? Some shrubs put on a spectacular display of color in the fall of the year, a final splash of glory that makes it possible to forgive them any shortcomings the rest of the time.

And, finally, consider the winter pattern of the trunks, branches and twigs. The silvery sheen of crape myrtle boughs, the interesting twist of the branches, the small brown seed pods, make this shrub attractive even when it is completely devoid of leaves. Many others share this quality when their branches are bare, so take note and keep this in mind when you plan your guest list. Handsome bark and twig color in winter is just as important as blossoms in spring.

Purposes

Suppose you want to hide some less-than-attractive area on your home grounds, such as a service yard. The friendly, quick-growing shrubs are your answer. Unlike trees, they can be planted close enough together to form a screen that effectively blots out the objectionable feature.

Low-growing shrubs form attractive border plants, making all the rest of the garden look neater and prettier because of their presence. Privet, along with the barberries, has long been considered the ideal hedge material and it is certainly well suited to the purpose. But don't limit yourself to the old standbys; there are dozens of others that stand pruning well. Some grow slowly and need little more than a bit of annual shaping. Others form light, open hedges which may be just what you need.

Some rambling, very low-growing shrubs, such as honeysuckle, make attractive ground covers, preventing erosion and nicely clothing steep banks which are difficult to mow. And shrubs do not require as much water as most plants, so they will survive better in periods of drought and in your absence. In fact, if you are gone for any length of time, you may find you have a lot of pruning to do when you return.

Yard Birds

By choosing the right shrubs, you can turn your garden into a haven for birds. They, along with the butterflies, add color and life to your garden, and, of course, birds are always happy to entertain you with a song. Shrubs, trees and vines are important in providing nesting places, affording the privacy birds want and need during the incubating and brooding periods. Remember, too, that there should be some insects in your garden, for these are gourmet treats to birds, whose presence keeps them from multiplying too rapidly. Shrubberies which produce berries are also attractive to birds—sometimes a bit too attractive, as in the case of the beautiful sapphireberry, which they feed on relentlessly until every last berry is gone. You might remember, however, that well-fed birds do less damage. So gain a little knowledge about the food preferences of different birds and put out a feeder. You may find that you can have both birds and berries.

In this case, a bird in the bush is worth quite a lot.

Flowers, fantastic foliage and free
fruit—all for you from the
smiling shrub family.

A gooseberry bush will provide flowers in the spring and fruit for pies and jelly in the summer.

Fruitful Fellows

Knowledgeable gardeners are no longer confining their planning to single-purpose shrubs. Beautiful blossoms are fine, but why not have fruit as well? Blueberries, elderberries, barberries, crab apples, flowering quince, currants, rosa rugosa, raspberries and many others have useful fruiting parts as well as lovely flowers. Include a few of these in your planting, and you will soon have material right on the home grounds for making your own wines and jellies.

And, whether you use these fruits or not, they are exceedingly attractive, adding another dimension to the shrub's usefulness as a decorative accent when the blooming season is past, often livening up the landscape during the winter months. The contrast of the brilliant red berries against white snow is an unforgettable sight, cheerful to behold on a cold and otherwise dreary day.

Beautiful Bargains

Of course shrubs are unexcelled for borders, or used as background material for annuals or perennials, but they can also be used alone.

If your time as well as your finances must be budgeted, flowering shrubs offer you an opportunity for beauty, color and fragrance, quick growth and minimal upkeep, unequaled by anything else in the plant kingdom.

Shrubs are fast growers and will spread out in no time at all, covering an area that would keep you busy watering and weeding if it were planted to annuals or perennials. They can deaden noise, hide a service or play yard, and provide you with privacy for patios and pools.

You can have all this and leisure too because most shrubs, especially those at home in your part of the country, aren't terribly particular about their living requirements. They can be quite happy in any soil that is reasonably fertile and well drained.

When the shrubs are young and just starting to grow, keep down the weeds. The youngsters shouldn't have to compete with them for food and water. As they grow older, many will shade the ground enough to overcome this problem by themselves.

LIGHTING YOUR SHRUBS

To get "overtime" enjoyment from your shrubs, consider a plan for lighting them.

Lights directed downward from a wall or fence will establish interesting patterns of light and shadow.

If you place lights below shrubs, focused upward, the plants are gracefully silhouetted against the night.

Parasol lamps can be used to illuminate small specimen plants and the area nearby. The downward cast of light is soft and pleasing. They also help to make your walkway safe.

For a special outdoor occasion you might try the fun idea of stringing small, all-white, Christmas-tree-type lights through your shrubs. This will give a subtle lighting effect and display leaves and branches glowing against the dark.

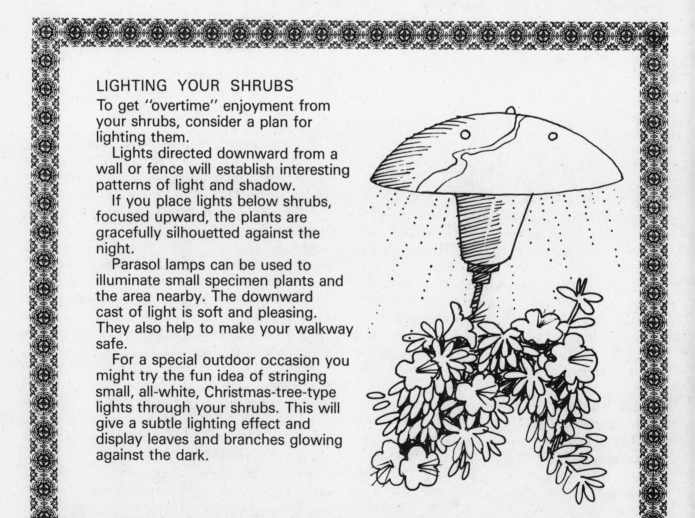

*This lilac is effectively used as
an accent to break up the expanse
of the white plaster wall behind it.*

Accentuate
the Positive

How you will prune your shrubs depends largely on how you plan to use them. Many grow naturally into well-shaped specimen plants, needing little training other than occasionally heading back a too-long branch, or removing old wood.

Consider just how large accent plants will become at maturity. If you can't allow a particular fellow all the room he needs, consider a yearly pruning (usually right after flowering), to keep him within bounds—or decide on something smaller. Many dwarfs, now available, take up less space and bloom more and longer than old-fashioned varieties.

There are some other pitfalls to avoid. Be sure you are getting exactly the right variety. Most nurseries are reliable and describe very carefully the type of stock they are offering, but sometimes you have to read between the lines and take note of what they do not say. There is, for instance, a whale of a difference between the European smoke tree and the native American one. The former is gorgeous, but the native type "smokes" very little. It is, however, far more brilliant in its fall suit. If you confuse the two, you may be in for a big disappointment.

Hedges may be any height, but if you are growing shrubs for a screen, they will quite likely be encouraged to attain their full potential. Some pruning may still be necessary, especially for the first few years, to keep them looking well. Give them much the same treatment as individual shrubs. Before you cut branches or stems, think ahead to how the plant will look when new shoots appear. Then prune the plant the way you want it to grow.

14

*A natural-looking border of azaleas
and rhododendrons gives unity
to this Oriental-style landscape.*

Border Boarders

Border plants usually need more pruning than other shrubs to give them the shape you want them to have. Cut border shrubs back to about 6 to 8 inches from the ground. Also cut the new shoots back to 6 to 8 inches from the old growth. Do this until the borders reach the desired thickness and height. Then, as new shoots appear, cut them back to a single bud. Prune your borders as often as necessary during the growing season.

Here's a hint worth knowing about. You can increase the number and size of flowers for the next year by removing seed pods as soon as they form. With flowering shrubs, always remember you should prune just as little and just as lightly as possible so they will always reward you with some flowers. Heavy pruning always reduces the number of blossoms.

Some leaf-losing shrubs bloom in spring and others in summer. Spring-flowering shrubs bloom until about mid-June; summer-flowering shrubs bloom from mid-June into fall. They are pruned at different times of the year and knowing "when" is important.

The blossoms of spring-flowering shrubs are formed on growth produced the previous year. If you prune these shrubs in the winter months, you will remove many of the flower buds that would produce blooms the following spring.

Spring-flowering fellows should be pruned as soon as the flowers fade and before new growth starts. Bear in mind that pruned plants will have larger blooms than unpruned ones.

BORDER SHRUBS

PRUNE NEW GROWTH 6-8 IN. TO MAKE BUSHY SHRUB

6-8"

PRUNE NEWLY PLANTED SHRUB

A few sprays of bridal-wreath spiraea will add grace and delicacy to a bouquet of larger flowers.

Cut Flowers

Properly conditioned flowers and foliage can often be made to last for weeks. Carry a container of water with you on your cutting expedition. You don't need much, just enough to partially immerse the stems so they will not dry out as you make other selections.

Use sharp clippers and cut cleanly. When cutting is completed, put the flowers in a cool room in a pail or bucket large enough to bring the water just up to, but not over, their chins. Leave them here for several hours or overnight.

Flowers with woody stems, such as most shrubs have, should be hammered an inch or two at the cut end to permit them to take up water more easily.

If you are preparing roses, strip off all the foliage and thorns that will be below the water line of the container. Thorns may be removed with a sharp knife or sand paper, but take care or a little mischief-maker may give you a sharp prick.

Blooms Cure Winter Gloom

Forcing branches to bloom in winter is one of the most rewarding off-season pleasures for gardeners and lovers of nature everywhere. I think more people would enjoy this hobby if they realized just how easy it is to do. Flower buds of spring-blooming shrubs and trees are fully formed in the fall. After a long winter's nap, the buds are all ready to grow when warmth and moisture are supplied.

Ordinarily, at least six weeks of cold temperature are required before flower buds awake. Thus, branches may be brought indoors for forcing at any time after the first of the new year.

Most shrubs have an abundance of buds along the younger shoots. Check for the large, plump ones—these are usually the flower buds, while the smaller ones are the leaves. Try to select branches that contain as many flower buds as possible. Look for "spurs" when selecting from quinces or ornamental crabs to force—it is on these short branches that they bear their flowers.

Don't do a lot of random cutting. Keep in mind where you will use these branches and what container you will put them in. This will avoid waste and help you select types and

Used alone, rhododendron makes a very dramatic floral arrangement.

lengths that will be most useful. Look at your material carefully, then select branches with interesting curves and angles.

Don't Be a Cut Up

Don't cut indiscriminately. Prune the branches you decide upon flush with the trunk or main branch so no stubs are left. And remember a clean, even cut will heal quickly with small danger of insect or disease damage. If you take branches larger than one inch in diameter, paint the exposed wound.

Do your cutting judiciously. Try to leave the plant more shapely after removing the branches you want. If your shrubs are still small take branches from several so that you will not rob any one of all its blossoms. No new buds will form as replacements for those removed.

Post-Operative Care

The cut stem will seal over, defeating your purpose, if you don't make it possible for the branches to absorb water by shredding or mashing the end of the stem. Using a hammer, pound an inch or two of the stem. If you live in a cold area, you must moisten the bud scales. (In warmer regions, this may not be necessary.) Soak the branches overnight in room temperature water. If you don't have a container that's large enough, use the bathtub. If that isn't feasible, wrap the tops with moistened burlap for several days.

After overnight soak, place the crushed ends in a bucket or other deep container for forcing. Add a piece of charcoal to keep the water sweet and change it once or twice a week.

Place the containers in a cool room to let the buds develop. Try to have the temperature around 60 to 65 degrees. Higher temperature will speed up the bud development, but you will have smaller flowers and less color, and they will not keep as well. It may even cause the buds to dry up and drop before they bloom.

It is not necessary to place them in the light during this stage. Just keep them in any convenient cool place. But watch carefully. As soon as the buds begin to "fatten," the branches should have light so the colors will develop. Do not, however, place them in the sun. Even in winter the heat may bring about rapid but poor development.

When the buds are nicely plump and a bit of color becomes evident, remove the branches from the pails. This should be done before they come into full bloom so there will be less likelihood of the flowers being bruised or broken.

Creating arrangements gives you a chance to display your artistic talents, so get together all the things you will need. If you have planned for this day in advance, you have probably gathered some other decorative material as well, such as pieces of moss, bark, pine cones, pebbles and, of course, vases and other containers.

Choose your containers with an eye to the branches that will grace them. The taller branches will look best in tall containers. Low bowls are excellent for vertical, L-shaped, or free-form designs. You can create a pleasing Oriental effect by using red Japanese quince. Arrange the deep red sprays in a low bowl, preferably black or some other dark color for contrast. The brilliant blossoms with their tiny, developing leaves just beginning to show are exquisite.

To keep your arrangements looking well as long as possible, move them to a cool room at night. Do this during the daytime if you are not at home to enjoy them and they will remain pretty much longer.

What can you force? Just about anything you want to. Any shrub that leafs out in early spring can be forced indoors. I like to vary my species and the time of cutting. By doing this I can have almost continuous bloom indoors until spring arrives.

SHRUBS IN CONTAINERS

You can enjoy the beauty of flowering shrubs even if your gardening space is limited to an apartment balcony or patio. Many of the loveliest flowering shrubs can be grown in containers.

Azaleas, especially the Belgian Indica and Kurume kinds, are the most popular shrubs for container culture and they are truly lovely. For an even more spectacular splash of color, try a tub-grown rhododendron on your porch. Both rhododendrons and azaleas do best in an acid, moist soil in a partially shaded location.

Crape myrtle, with its crepe-paper-like blossoms and brilliant autumn foliage, will adapt itself to growing in a container. (The dwarf forms are best for this purpose.) The big-leaf hydrangea is another excellent choice. Its giant clusters of white or pastel flowers are a welcome sight on a summer day.

Large, unglazed clay pots, wooden tubs, barrel halves and concrete urns are among the containers you might use. Whatever you choose, remember to water and feed your shrub regularly to compensate for its limited growing area.

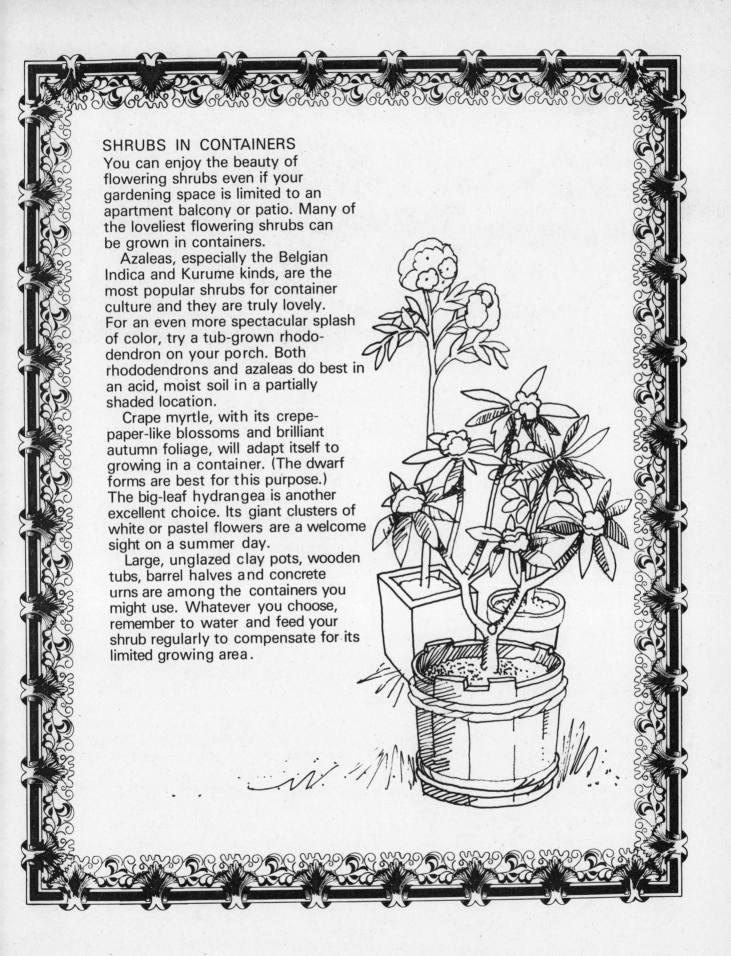

Season of Bloom

Every season has its own special flavor. What you plant to achieve the most from your material depends to a large extent on the section of the country where you live. There are no hard and fast rules that apply to every area.

Shredding leaves is a habit many shrubs learn when they come in contact with cold winters. They may be evergreen in the South; farther North the leaves may shrivel but continue to cling. In a still colder area, they may deepen to reds and gold, then finally turn a russet brown and drop off.

The gay colors painted by autumn are not, as many think, attributable to frost. Frost may hasten the process but the shrub, a clever fellow, is pulling carbohydrates and other materials back into the leaf. These are gradually withdrawn into his twigs and from there into his trunk and finally into his roots for safekeeping during the period of cold that he knows is on its way.

If you live in an area where the atmosphere is moist, the colors of autumn leaves are apt to be less vivid than in warmer, drier sections. Long, dry fall days are most productive of brilliant color. The sparkling scarlets and glittering golds appear long before the first frost. Even this is not always "for sure." Cold rains may fade the colors and spoil the scene for that particular year. An unexpected sharp freeze may cut the leaves off before they ripen. But if none of these things happens, you will get a glorious display in autumn as many of your favorite shrubs ripen their leaves and berries.

And berrying characteristics are just as important to shrub beauty as the flowers—sometimes more important. I have a special affection for the friendly berry bearers who perk up the winter landscape. They often do even more to cheer me up during the cold, dreary days than their flowers do in the spring. That sprinkling of bright crimson berries against the monotony of pines and cedars really sparks up my day.

There are even winter flowers. A few dull leaves may still cling to the witch hazel, and against these, the elfin flowers shine like threads of gold.

In time, the winter winds will tear the red robes from all the trees, leaving only the bare branches. But even then, the bark and twisted twigs make patterns of light and shade.

Then, as you watch from day to day, you will begin to notice shining buds appearing, promising that the legend of summer will be retold in a few short months. Cheer up—spring will surely come again just when you need it most.

Many shrubs are ornamental all year round, even in winter when they display interesting branching patterns and ornamental berries.

Buying

Make friends with your nurseryman! He can give you lots of valuable advice.

Every time I think about shopping for plants, I think of Cheap John's, a joint that made its owner rich by selling low-quality, out-of-style clothes to college boys. At a glance, everyone knew which slacks and coats came from Cheap John's, and Cheap John's customers had to return twice as often as those who patronized the better clothing stores. I'm not knocking bargains, mind you, but the quality of a product shows, and

how much wear and tear it can take often determines if it's really a good buy. That goes for clothes as well as flowering shrubs.

Before you think about actually shopping for your shrubs, you ought to know what you want. Do you need a few flowering shrubs for a small yard, or a lot of them to hide your backyard all cluttered up with Junior's toys? I know you're not surprised to hear me say that you ought to plan ahead. Know what you want before you even approach your nurseryman for advice.

If you're going flowering-shrubs shopping on Thursday, and your paper-bag plan reveals an empty spot under the picture window in the den, then know what you're going shopping for. You might not know the name of the shrub, so tell the nurseryman, "I want a flowering shrub that will grow in full sunlight which will not grow taller than four feet, but will branch out five feet and has greenery all year long." Chances are, he'll have a shrub in mind before you finish giving your order.

As you choose your quality plants from a reputable dealer, keep in mind the permanency of your purchase. Shrub buying, like marriage, should be for a lifetime. So look before you leap, and be sure that you really want that forsythia before you buy it a one-way ticket to your front yard.

When choosing your plants, don't forget for a minute that over-all effect you want to achieve. The wrong shrub will stand out like a sore thumb at a manicurists' convention.

If you want your yard to look like the grounds of Windsor Castle, go ahead and buy only formal flowering shrubs, but if you want an informal, cozy atmosphere, choose shrubs to match. Don't have a yard full of neatly trimmed flowering shrubs and stick in one shaggy bush that you have no intention of giving regular hair cuts.

You might go a step beyond my paper-bag plan if you own a Polaroid camera. Make color pictures of your home from every possible angle. When you go shopping for shrubs, you can't drag your house along, so take the pictures with you. That way, the nurseryman can get acquanted with the house and figure out what would look attractive with it.

An insurance salesman told me that the greatest damage done to his car in a year's time is by unkept, thorny shrubs that scar cars for a hobby. Your drive should be kept free of overhanging or fruiting shrubs. Fruit-bearing shrubs ought to be planted in a help-yourself area. And, please, don't plant overgrown, bushy shrubs where they'll attack people who have to back out of your drive, which is difficult enough as it is. If you have a corner lot, save your huge bushes for someplace besides the corner itself, where they endanger lives by blocking traffic views

One final word of caution—especially if you want to stay on good terms with your neighbor. Don't plant mimosas or other messy shrubs or trees where they will hang over the shed on his drive. I often wonder how many friendships have been ruined over trees and shrubs planted on boundary lines. Know what your plants will do so that you can control their behavior and keep your neighbors happy.

Bogus Bargains

I love to look at beautiful, flowering shrubs in catalogs. But I don't let my enthusiasm overcome my good sense. And neither should you. Do not deal with a nursery that is not well-established and well-proven. Call your state agricultural department for information on catalog dealers.

If you want to risk ordering from a nursery that seems to offer fantastic bargains, go ahead. You might have to learn the hard way. Fly-by-night nurseries will risk what reputations they've got by sending poor-quality shrubs. No reputable nursery will send you a shrub that will hurt his reputation. The lesser-known catalog dealers often send a brochure or catalog to every patron on every street in every house in the USA. His fancy advertisements and colorful pictures are bound to fool at least a few people. Most of these nursery houses of ill repute know that an experienced gardener will immediately realize that you can't get quality plants at the ridiculously low prices some catalogs offer. I recently saw a brochure that advertised nearly $25 worth of rhododendron, forsythia, pussy willow and crape myrtle bushes for less than $5! I laughed all the way to the trash can. It's a real shame that lots of unsuspecting shrub shoppers will get the wrong impression of some of the world's most beautiful plants because of a bad bargain nursery.

Beware of any advertisement that sounds too good to be true. It usually is. Sometimes, however, a well-established dealer will offer pre-season prices that are lower than usual. You get a bonus for ordering ahead of the busiest season. Sometimes he will also offer better prices when you buy several shrubs of the same kind.

Unless you're dealing with a reputable, well-established catalog firm, go to your local nursery for your flowering shrubs. Not only will you be able to see what you're buying, but you can ask all kinds of questions. For some reason, most nurserymen are unusually patient people. They have to put up with short growing seasons, even shorter seasons in which to move their products, and a lot of people who don't know a daphne from a dogwood.

Some gardeners are afraid to visit a nursery just to window shop. I encourage it because it is a cheap way of spending an afternoon and because you can pick up a lot of good ideas. Maybe you're considering a flowering dogwood for your new flower garden, but your wife doesn't agree with your choice. Suddenly, on a Friday afternoon at the local nursery you see a tree holly that would be even better for that spot. You buy it and find that your wife loves it too. One browsing trip to the nursery has saved your marriage, beautified your garden and provided you with an entertaining afternoon.

Choosing

An educated shopper is hard to fool. You don't need a degree in agriculture to be able to distinguish a good plant from a poor one.

When I say "good" plant, I mean one with many virtues. A plant could be perfectly healthy, but if it's wrong for your landscaping scheme, it isn't a good choice for you.

Once you've decided on what your yard and house need, think about the actual condition of the plant itself. If you went to a pet shop to choose a dog, you'd be furious if the owner showed you a sickly animal. Likewise, general good health is the first thing you look for in a flowering shrub. But how can you tell a sick plant from a healthy one? When in doubt, consult your nurseryman. Better still, learn what healthy plants look like.

To begin with, a healthy shrub doesn't look sick. It has no leaf spots, stem cankers, or sores. So if Aunt Ethel offers to give you one of her dubious-looking shrubs, tell her you'd rather do without until you find one that doesn't look like it has chicken pox.

Look for a shrub that has been grown in a full circle of light. Shrubs grown with light on only one side look undeveloped on the other. That's why you always turn when you sunbathe rather than burn in some spots and stay white in others.

Look at the feet of the shrubs. The roots of a healthy plant will not be swollen. Swelling usually means disease, and who wants a plant

"We pledge to be a good hedge."

that has varicose veins before it even starts standing in your yard?

A healthy plant has good posture and full foliage. Its sideburns, or side-branch growth, are not thin and puny-looking, but full and close to the ground. Avoid knotty knees in a young plant—with age the condition will worsen.

I don't actually carry a magnifying glass around in my pocket, but I do look to see if the trunks of shrubs are shriveled or wrinkled. Dead twigs, brown leaves, and wrinkled bark show signs of aging. Most likely the plant has dried out from neglect, and hasty watering and feeding have made it look passable again. But I would not want it to live with me.

Also look closely at the new growth on flowering shrubs. Is it very soft yellow-green in color? If so, your plant probably got left in a room that was far too hot and too dark and was then put outside where it nearly froze to death.

Check for insects, too, though high-quality nurseries usually keep pests away from their plants. Look for white cottony masses and gray patches on the stems of the shrubs. If you find any, tell the nurseryman that his plants need de-bugging.

Don't feel sorry for sick plants at the nursery. Try to hint to the dealer that the honeysuckle needs perking up a little, but don't let him talk you into taking it home with you. The little darling may look precious, but he might be carrying a disease or pest that could cost you a pretty penny if it spreads. When you're looking at new babies for your yard, admire them all, but think health when you're ready to take one home to Mama.

Winners All the Way

It's hard to pick a loser when it comes to flowering shrubs. They are beautiful, they spread rapidly to cover a much larger area in a shorter time than evergreens, and they are very versatile.

They fit in the ecological picture perfectly. They control noise by acting as a living wall. I've seen forsythia and spiraea used as anti-noise plantings. Prune them so they'll grow thick instead of tall.

Many houses in the city face an alley in the back and the street in the front. The back usually poses the biggest problems because of outbuildings, often necessary for storage or pets. With proper use of flowering shrubs, you can even fool the milkman into thinking it's a florist's hideout and not a storage area. Japanese dogwood that fans out to 25 by 12

A clump of bamboo will do a good job of camouflaging garbage cans, pet yards or other unsightly areas.

feet is great for camouflaging. Against white outbuildings, I like the cotoneasters which spread out horizontally and call attention to themselves rather than the buildings.

Instead of unsightly buildings, maybe you have children you can't keep in the yard. I've seen many children climb a $200 chain-link fence, even with prongs on top, but I've yet to see a kiddy scale a $20 Japanese privet hedge that's thick at the bottom and about 5 feet high. Red spiraea, boxwood, forsythia and multiflora rosa also make pretty hedges, and if you can keep your kids quiet, your neighbors won't even see them—or the bicycle frames, roller skates and chewed-up tennis shoes the children are going to pick up tomorrow.

If you have children, you probably have dogs. You don't have to hedge in your whole backyard to keep them from rampaging through the neighborhood. Just box in an area large enough to give them proper exercise.

If you don't want a redwood fence or a look-see swimming pool enclosure, hedge in your patio area with lilac or with the old stand-bys, forsythia or spiraea. In the South, you might use crape myrtle.

If you like birds, you can plant food for them by buying shrubs in the berry family. Edible fruits luscious enough to tempt the most particular gourmet can be on hand for your enjoyment, too.

Color is one of the most important things to consider in choosing flowering shrubs. If you are carrying out a definite color scheme in your yard, you need to plan each purchase carefully.

If you stop to think about it, there aren't many months of the year when flowers can really dress up in their bright colors. Most of the time they have to wear their basic greens. Well, if you're interested in flowering shrubs, you're in for a treat because their year-round uniforms are often as pretty as their new spring frocks. As a matter of fact, I have some friends who cherish the foliage of their bottlebrush buckeye more than the blossoms the plants produce.

Weigelas grow 9 to 10 feet tall,
so be sure to give them
lots of room to grow in.

Growing Pains

When you buy a shrub, make absolutely sure you know how large it's going to get before you take it home. It's also a good idea to measure the spot you have in mind for it before you leave home. If, for example, you want something to plant in front of a fairly low window, don't buy a spicebush just because you liked a picture you saw in a magazine. If you do a little research beforehand, you'll learn that spicebushes often reach 15 feet height. Unless you like your shrubs to press their noses against the window pane and blot out the sun, you'd do better with something smaller—perhaps a Japanese barberry.

Suppose you have a bald spot right behind your garage. No one ever sees it but you every time you empty the trash. What can you put there that will be pretty and large? The weigela is just your child. Wand Weigela grows about 8 feet tall, has coarse dark-green foliage and pink or white fragrant flowers. When she's all dressed up in her spring finery, you may find that you don't mind taking out the garbage—at least not as much as usual.

Weather Worries

You can force many flowering shrubs to grow in bad conditions, but they usually pay for it with their lives. Or else they are sickly children who demand constant attention—and you know how doctor bills mount up!

Climate is a combination of temperature, humidity, sunshine, wind, air pressure, and precipitation. Mother Nature usually throws in a few tornadoes and storms here and there, too. Some plants cannot survive a climate unlike that of their natural habitat. The gardenia, for example, won't grow in a cold,

outdoor climate. Geraldine Gardenia has to have a mild climate, which means she would be happy in parts of California and Texas but miserable in New England—except indoors. I understand her warm nature and wouldn't dream of treatening her with exposure to the cold.

Some flowering shrubs like dampness, but all want good drainage. Summer sweet will tolerate damp feet but not extreme cold.

Since I know that honeysuckle will grow almost anywhere above the Gulf States, I can take her a lot of places my other children couldn't go. Her eating habits are great, too, as she will gorge herself on almost any soil. Her fragrance is, of course, unsurpassed.

Since you cannot control climate and probably don't want to move just to please your shrubs, you must select shrubs that will do well where you live. Don't expect miracles from your nurseryman. He might be persuaded to sell you a plant that he knows will not thrive in your area if you're persistent enough, but he knows that you'll be better satisfied with plants that like where you live.

You can change soil conditions to some extent, and you can control the sun by planting in the shade, but you can't tamper very much with Mother Nature. Be flexible in buying plants and don't insist on the ridiculous. You can force your shrub to grow in a foreign climate—maybe—but in the heart of that dear flower child, it will be back in its own hometown.

If you're puzzled about what to grow where you live, ask your nurseryman or extension agent. Tell them I sent you!

Rather than fussing with exotic, rare children who are difficult to raise, stick with the favorites in your area. Give me several healthy spiraeas rather than one unusual shrub that has to be babied all winter long with foliage colic.

Super-Charged Shrubs

Deciding which flowering shrubs are best for you is something like buying a new car. First of all, you want service and dependability, no matter what car you end up buying. But you don't consider just those factors. You also think about color, passenger load, extras, size and the over-all impression you want to make on your neighbors.

With flowering shrubs, you want to consider what will grow best in your own climate first of all. Then you can think about more specific matters. Is your soil acid enough for azaleas? If not, what can you do to correct

the problem? Is a particular shrub going to grow too tall if I plant it under my kitchen windows?

You must also consider the other plants and trees in your yard. Choose shrubs that complement your landscape. Learn how to use accent pieces effectively. Don't fill your yard with randomly planted individual shrubs.

You have to consider expense, too. Unless you have a lot of money, you'll want to investigate prices before picking out shrubs. I'd rather have a few beautiful, long-lasting flowering shrubs than a yard full of cheap, mediocre plants.

A Happy Home

Flowering shrubs, spoiled children though they are, don't fuss much about their beds. They just like a well-drained soil without weeds. However, some do prefer shade while others prefer sun. It's useless to try to grow plants without getting to know them. Read up on the peculiarities of your particular flowering shrubs. Learn what they like to eat, whether they're sun lovers, and which kind words and phrases send them into orbit. Don't make the mistake one man did when his wife accused him of never calling her by the pet name he used when they were courting 30 years earlier. He thought and thought and finally remembered. He hurried home, hugged her tight, and whispered in loving tones, "I love you, you old nanny goat!" After his head wound healed, she told him that the term of endearment had been "little lambie pie"! Your plants will be just as angry as that wife if you call them by another shrub's name.

Most shrubs prefer the sun, but some do well in the shade. If you have a shady, bald spot that needs a flowering shrub, try one of these: bush honeysuckle, azalea, rhododendron, barberry, blueberry, deutzia, pussy willow, spice bush, mountain-laurel, and kerria. As a general rule, shrubs which naturally grow in woodlands will prefer shade to full sun. Studying the natural habitat of your shrubs will give you a better idea of where they want to live.

City Slickers

Raise your hand if you live in the city or suburbs. Look at all those hands! Well, you've got to have something to make your yard attractive whether it's a narrow strip of poor soil or a spacious, fertile lot. Let me warn you, though, that you'll have to prepare for some problems that the country squire won't have.

City soil is not usually very rich. Light and sun are almost unheard of by some city residents today. Drainage is seldom good. Smoke and gas fumes annoy plants immensely. Buildings often make too much shade. And you're lucky if you've got room to plant a daisy, to say nothing of a forsythia.

But you can overcome all these obstacles if your love is true. Some of the prettiest spots in New York City are the windowboxes that sparkle with color and defy every law of pollution.

I'll be honest and tell you that evergreens don't care much for the city because, like us, they find it difficult to breathe with the air full of soot and dust. However, some plants have been cultivated to tolerate city conditions. Besides general shrub health, you'll have to consider size, too. If you don't own your home, condominium, or apartment, you'll have to get permission before planting shrubs. Shrubs and trees, more than anything else, increase the value of property, so sell your landlord on the idea. Let him know how valuable your contribution to his property will be.

Forsythia is a real city slicker, and even mountain laurel will grow in town if you'll wash it now and then. I give my children showers about every 3 weeks. We sing together while I shower them down, usually "It Only Hurts for a Little While." They didn't like their showers at first, but they've gradually learned to love them. They're grateful when I'm finished, because their crawly insects are gone and they can breathe deeply once again.

One of the best flowers for a city garden is the showy, fragrant snow azalea. It usually blooms in spite of dust, soot, and gases when other members of the rhododendron family won't. Deutzia and flowering quince are city lovers. I've also taken many mock-oranges to the city, and once they've seen the lights, they don't want to return to the farm. Some of the lilacs will grow in cities and add fragrance and beauty to dreary streets.

For the loveliest lawn on the block, find out what shrubs do well in your area and plant lots of them.

High and Dry

There's something for everybody in the flowering-shrub kingdom. Even if you live in a dry area, there are some which will gladly grace your yard with their presence. Not very many shrubs really ask for dry living conditions, but some have peculiar tastes. Beauty bush doesn't mind heat and wind and actually enjoys dry soil. It produces beautiful pink bells with yellow "ringers" inside. The gray-green foliage has a hairy texture.

The hardy silver berry (Elaeagnus commutata) prefers dry conditions, too. Sally silver berry is very leggy, but she has great posture and grows up to 10 feet tall. She's drought-resistant and hardy but you'd never know it. In late spring and summer, when Sally decks herself out in fragrant, yellow flowers which are followed by delicate silvery berries, she's as beautiful as any of her more delicate sisters.

Tamarix looks great in a bikini down at the seashore. Her flowers are feathery and can be taken indoors for floral arrangements. Tammy even likes the feel of salt spray and wind in her face. If you own a summer cottage at the seashore, take Tammy Tamarix with you. She's a real lifesaver at the beach.

Vive la Différence!

Different plants like different soils, so no blanket statement can be made to cover every situation. You'll have to think ahead in choosing soil and sites for your shrubs. Shady soil is not like sunny soil. For example, water affects shady and sunny areas differently. Before you decide on a plant, you also need to test the acidity of the areas. Some plants, such as azaleas, love acid soil, and you'll hurt their feelings if you put them elsewhere.

Sandy soils will have to be treated with organic materials to improve their water-handling capacity. The same treatment improves the drainage of clayey soil.

You can't expect to grow plants that like moisture in soil that has the water-holding capacity of a sieve. I've seen good money literally poured down the drain by people who planted flowering shrubs in soils with severe drainage problems.

If you don't know if you have good soil drainage—one of the most important requirements for bountiful flowers of all kinds—make the rain test. Actually, you can just use a couple of gallons of water, but it's more fun to invite a kid outside with you in a good rain. If the water seeps into the soil at a casual rate and soaks down about a foot deep, chances are your drainage is good. If the water runs off the ground without soaking in or stands in puddles, you are in need of a good drain doctor.

I'm going to tell you how to plant various flowering shrubs, but no instructions are going to keep your plant healthy if your basic soil is sick. Most flowering shrubs prefer light, loose soil with good drainage. Work your soil until it yells stop—at least twice as deep as the roots of your plant. I always add a good helping of 60-40 gravel to the existing soil if it's clayey.

Your shrubs will never produce gorgeous flowers like the one above if they're drowning in poorly drained soil.

Planting

The time to plant flowering shrubs is any time you can get a shovel in the ground. Most people plant their shrubs in fall or early spring. If you buy healthy plants with well-protected roots, you can play around with planting time a little.

Bare-rooted shrubs ought to be put to bed after the foliage is gone but before new buds start swelling. Remember to watch for this sign the next time you visit a nursery. If the dealer has been keeping the plants in shade, don't stick them in full sunlight immediately. You don't want them to get sunstroke, do you?

Let me give you my simple formula for planting flowering shrubs. It works for me and for all my friends who call me wanting to know when to plant something they've already bought at a rummage sale! You see that I've drawn a line across the map of the United States. If you live south or west of that line, you can plant flowering shrubs all winter long. North of the line, plant your shrubs in spring or early fall.

Dig In

Planting flowering shrubs is more than digging a hole, dropping the plant in, and kicking a little soil around it. First, you should take a close look at the containers your new shrubs live in. Shrubs come in three different kinds of containers—balled-in burlap, metal containers, and plantable paper-pulp pots. You can also purchase bare-root plants. Look closely at the container. If, for example, you have found a lovely spiraea, but the ball of soil around it is loose leave it alone. It will probably die of root shock because the soil has fallen away from the roots. Likewise, don't buy any plants in split paper-pulp containers, or in loose, wobbly metal containers.

When possible, plant your shrubs as soon as you arrive home. I'd feel terrible if you invited me to your house and left me sitting in your driveway. Don't show such rudeness to your plants either.

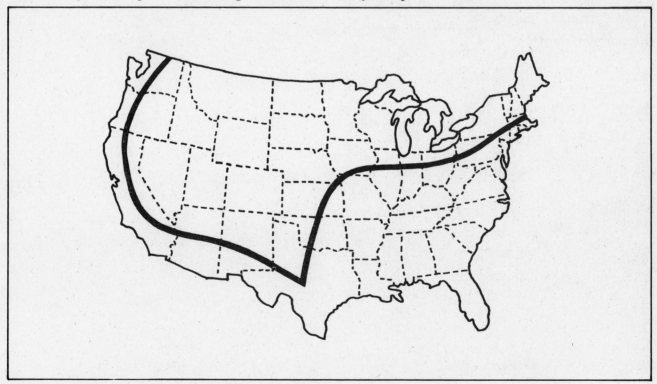

Don't cramp your shrub's style by poking it in a too-small hole. Have you ever heard of digging a five-dollar hole for a fifty-cent plant? That means digging a hole half again as wide as the width of the container and 6 inches deeper than the height. You don't want to smother the plant roots, though, by planting it more than an inch or so deeper than it was originally. Put enough loose soil in the bottom of the hole to raise the plant to the correct depth.

If you can't plant your shrubs immediately, be sure to make them comfortable until you can. The best way to do this is by heeling them in. Heeling-in is particularly useful for unexpected arrivals from catalog dealers.

Dig a trench in a well-drained area. (If the word "trench" scares you, call it a shallow ditch.) Cut one side straight down, deep enough for the roots to sit in comfortably. Cut the other side on a slant.

Lay your plants so that the stems are leaning on the slope and their roots are touching the verticle wall. Put them close together so they can snuggle up to their old friends. Completely cover the roots and give them a long drink of water before saying good-night. If you plan to leave your shrubs in the trench until spring, gently firm the dirt around the roots and cover the stems and lowest branches, too.

"He thinks he's the star of 'Bare-Root in the Park.'"

1

Dig a hole 6 inches wider all around than the roots. Use a mixture of 2 parts topsoil and 1 part peat moss to make a mound in the bottom of the hole. Set the shrub on the mound and spread the roots. Lay a board across the hole to make sure the shrub is set at the same depth it was at the nursery.

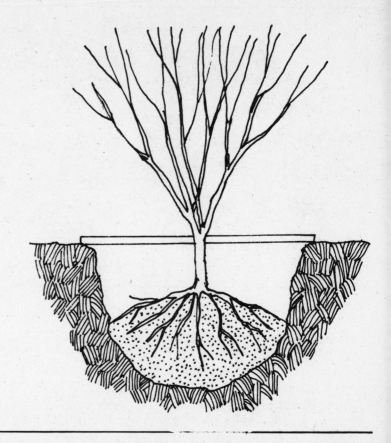

3

Finish filling the hole and mound up a low dam around it. Water thoroughly again. Finally prune back the branches by about a third to compensate for any damage to the roots.

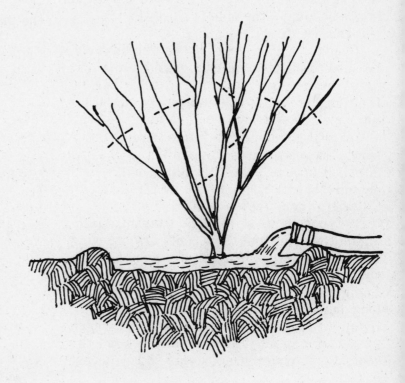

2

Fill the hole ¾ full with the soil and peat moss mixture. Carefully firm the soil with your foot, then fill the hole with water and let it soak in.

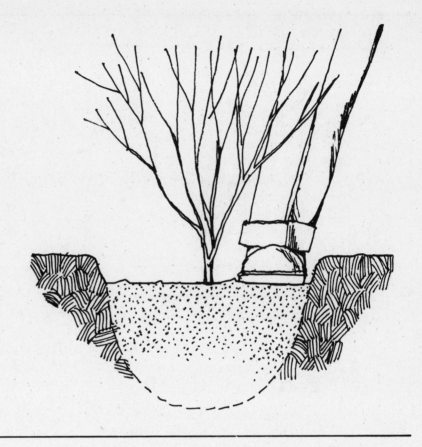

Burlapped Shrubs Are a Ball

In the past, most nurserymen balled and burlapped their shrubs, but the skill of balling shrubs is becoming extinct. Balling a shrub is a true art which requires skill, speed and experience. If the person balling your shrub mishandles it, your chances of raising it are very slim.

Very tenderly put your new plant into its hole. Settle it in with a firm, but gentle hand.

Walk away from it and survey the results. Is the plant straight or does it need a little adjustment? If the plant's posture is poor, carefully lift it from the hole and adjust the bottom of the hole. Don't be satisfied until your shrub stands straight and tall. Give it a start in life that will make it reach for the sky with pride, not hang its limbs in shame.

When the plant is settled, unfasten the burlap at the top. Cut the loose pieces away if you like, but be careful not to disturb the soil around the roots. I usually just leave the burlap right where it is once I've removed the nails at the top. The burlap will soon decay and in the meantime it'll make a good security blanket for your young shrubs.

With your plant in place, refill the hole with your mixture of sandy gravel and garden soil. When the hole is half full, pack the soil down with your foot so you'll have no air pockets. Fill the hole with water to further settle the soil. Gradually, finish filling up the hole.

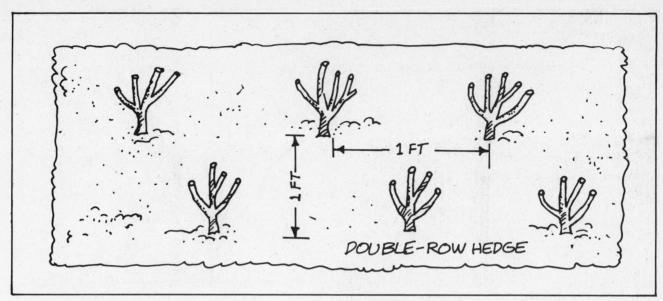

DOUBLE-ROW HEDGE

Spacing for Hedges

You probably think of a hedge as being a living fence and that was once the primary purpose of it, but in less formal gardens nowadays, hedges are often used to create illusions. You might want your short garden spot to appear longer, and a narrow hedge would do the trick. A hedge can become a barrier to keep out rascals or a screen to hide your garbage cans.

Plants for hedges should be hardy and able to withstand whatever comes along. If one hedge plant is killed off in the winter, you're left with a gap in the hedge row. A new plant will take forever to reach a decent size.

Spacing between individual hedge plants is decided by the type of plant and how large you want it to grow. Generally, hedge plants are set between 1 and 3 feet apart. If you're planning a double hedge, you must leave about a foot of space between rows.

Since hedge plants grow so close together and must compete for available food, you need to make sure the soil is rich. If you have a family, you expect to provide more food for them than you would for yourself alone. Likewise, an individual forsythia can live off far less food than a bunch of forsythia plants in a hedge.

Burning-bush makes a good hedge providing both fruit and a spectacular display of scarlet foliage in autumn. It only grows about 4 feet tall, so you can still chat with your neighbors over it, and you seldom have to give this obedient child a haircut.

I like forsythia, even if it is considered quite common. It's one of the earliest shrubs to flower in spring, and it makes a pretty informal hedge. I've used these golden beauties on steep banks where they look lovely and save me a lot of mowing. For one of the showiest gardens in town, plant a forsythia hedge and in front of it make a bed of spring-flowering bulbs—tulips, daffodils, grape-hyacinths or scillas. Forsythia is easy to grow and very few pests like it—except the two-legged one who might break off some branches for floral arrangements.

Japanese white spiraea is a dense, compact shrub that produces showy white flowers. If you like red better than white, plant the spiraea with scarlet blossoms. There's no prettier flowering hedge than this, and the leaves are thick and attractive when the blossoms are gone.

Shrub roses and privet are both popular as hedges. The roses are thorny, of course, but their lovely, fragrant blossoms more than make up for this minor drawback.

Care of Newly Planted Shrubs

There are some procedures that will help you get your newly planted or transplanted shrubs off to a good start. It is essential that you cut back the bare-root shrubs at least a third of the way when they are first planted. I do the same with my potted and balled-in-burlap shrubs. Moving a plant to a new home causes a loss of moisture. Cutting back the branches will help the shrub adjust to this loss.

I never feed my newly planted shrubs right away. No one is in shape for a big, formal meal right after moving day, so let your shrubs wait a couple of weeks. Let them get used to their new soil neighbors. After a couple of weeks, you can give them one of the fish-emulsion fertilizers. After a month, feed them again with a low-nitrogen, dry garden food, either 4-12-4 or 5-10-5. This will speed up root growth.

I also mulch the roots of my newly planted shrubs with wood chips. Lay them on about 2 inches deep and spread them as far as the bottom branches extend. Besides keeping down weeds, mulching will hold moisture in the soil.

Flowering-shrub hedges are less formal than evergreen hedges and are therefore better suited to modern landscapes.

Canny Shrubs

If you buy a shrub in a metal container, have the container cut on one side from top to bottom. Don't pick up the shrub by the stem or you might shake soil away from the roots. Instead, remove the metal can carefully.

After removing the plant from its container, put it to bed as you did your bur-lapped shrubs. I always try to determine a shrub's best profile, then I put that side forward.

Plants in paper-pulp containers are the easiest to set out as you are less likely to damage their roots.

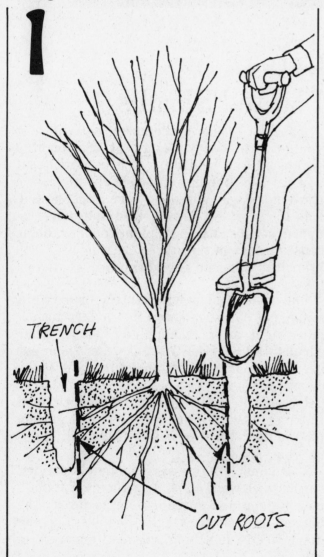

TRENCH

CUT ROOTS

Carefully slice the four sides of the paper-pulp container if it's square. If it's round, make several slits around the cup. Gently set the whole cup into the hole, supporting the container, with your hands beneath it. Holding onto the sides of the cup could loosen the soil. Once planted, the paper pulp cup will decompose.

Moving Day

Moving an established shrub is no easy task, so I don't have to tell you that you should transplant shrubs only if you have very good reasons. If you move them on a whim, they'll resent it and you'll regret it.

The best time for transplanting is early fall or very early spring when the evenings are cool. Moving a shrub during hot weather would make both you and the shrub un-comfortable.

Don't try to move a shrub that is really huge. Call a professional tree mover instead.

Some prepping is necessary before you move your shrubs. I tie mine up with old nylon hose to hold the foliage snugly in place. This will keep you from breaking branches and save your face from some nasty scratches.

Water the shrub the night before you plan to move it, and explain what's going on. Be sure to get the soil damp enough so that it will stick to the roots on moving day.

The next day, dig a hole for your new shrub, preparing it as you would for an ordinary planting. Be sure your tools are razor sharp before you dig up the shrubs. A dull shovel will damage the roots.

How do you determine just how much soil to take with your shrub? The size of the shrub and its root system determines that. The older and larger the plant, the more soil you'll need.

Dig straight down with your spade, cutting through the roots cleanly. Circle the plant. Complete your circle, then dig a trench all the way around the circle. Make the trench twice

1. If you want to move a shrub to a new location in your yard, start by digging a trench twice as deep as your spade is long around the shrub. Dig a slight ramp.

2. Now dig beneath the soil ball. Place the end of a piece of heavy cardboard under the soil ball. Carefully pull the shrub onto the cardboard, and slide it out of the hole and to its new home.

3. Place a layer of compost or peat moss in the bottom of the new planting hole. Set the new plant at the proper depth, half-fill the hole and water thoroughly. Finish filling the hole, water again and spread on a layer of mulch.

as deep as the blade of your spade is long. Then with your back to the new location of the shrub, dig a slight ramp up and away from the soil ball so that you can slide the shrub out easily.

Carefully dig beneath the soil ball. Gently rock the plant to see if it is free. Place one end of a large piece of cardboard under the edge of the ball. Pull the plant onto the cardboard, then gently pull cardboard, plant and all out of the hole. Carefully slide the cardboard along until it is next to the new home.

Slide the shrub into its new hole as gently as possible. Be sure the shrub is sitting at the right angle before refilling the hole.

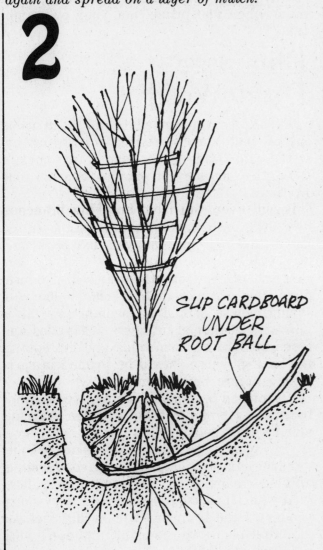

2

SLIP CARDBOARD UNDER ROOT BALL

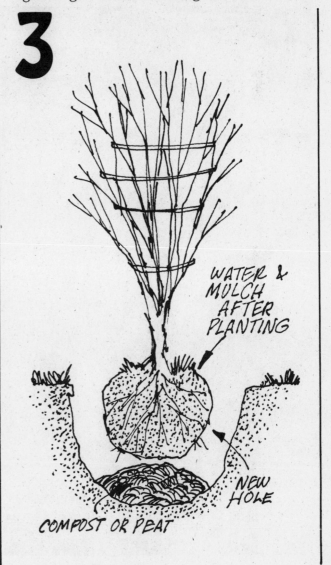

3

WATER & MULCH AFTER PLANTING

NEW HOLE

COMPOST OR PEAT

Pruning

Shrubs are pruned because they need it, not just because of looks—even though prettier shrubs are one of the by-products of correct pruning. Sometimes your shrubs will have to be cut back drastically to make them flower properly or simply because everything seems to have gone wrong. Nothing, however, makes my heart bleed more than seeing a shrub that's meant to have wide, open arms cut down to the quick. Always keep the health of your shrubs in mind when you prune, not your own ambitions.

Eliminate Dead Wood

Sometimes you'll need to cut dead wood out of your shrubs. Aside from being unattractive, dead wood saps your shrub's strength. This sort of pruning can be done anytime.

If you're removing live wood, you'll have to be a little more careful about timing. If you prune at the wrong time, you just might end up with a shapely shrub and no flowers. Some shrubs, such as forsythias and lilacs, form buds the summer before they bloom in spring. These should be pruned soon after flowering. Other shrubs, crape myrtles and roses of Sharon, form buds and blossom in the spring. These should be pruned in early spring before buds form.

Cut out all branches that rub across other branches. If you don't, the weaker branches will be damaged.

I'm against pruning azaleas or rhododendron unless it is absolutely, unquestionably necessary. If you have to prune azaleas, do it when they are in bloom. Use very sharp shears so the branches will hardly feel the cut. Mulch beneath the plants and don't cultivate around them.

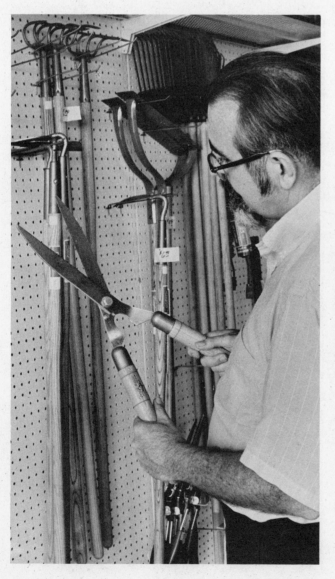

*"That wasn't nearly as bad as
I thought it would be."*

Shrub	When to Prune	How to Prune
Azaleas	After flowering	Prune lightly, shaping and thinning
Barberries	Spring	Thin as necessary
Blueberries	Late fall or early spring	Remove lateral shoots and thin as necessary
Butterfly Bushes	Spring	Cut back to within 2 or 3 inches of old wood
Cotoneasters	After berries fall	Cut out old shoots and shape new growth
Crape myrtles	Before growth starts in spring	Cut out dead branches and thin as necessary
Forsythias	After flowering	Cut oldest branches back to ground level
Hydrangeas	Early spring	Head back
Kerrias	After flowering	Cut back old branches and thin as necessary
Korean Abelialeaf	Spring	Thin as necessary
Lilacs	After flowering	Remove suckers at ground level and thin
Mock Oranges	After flowering	Cut back 1/3 of old canes
Quinces	Early summer after flowering	Shape and thin
Viburnums	Spring	Thin and shape as necessary

Early spring is the best time to prune out weak, diseased, broken or dead branches. Shrubs that flower on the current season's growth can also be shaped at this time. Cut back 1/3 of the oldest stems to 3 inches above the ground.

If a shrub is badly overgrown, or very leggy, cut every branch back to within 2 to 5 inches of the ground. The best time for doing this is early spring.

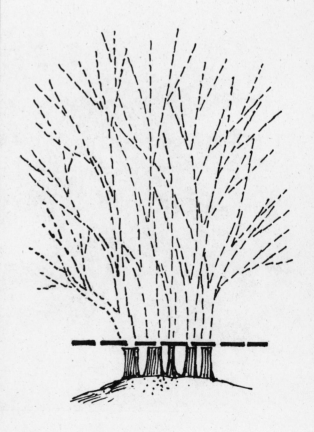

Time for a Haircut

Keep an eye on those flower children of yours. When it appears that they are having growing pains, you may need to consider pruning. Look at the shoots grown since last season. Are they large enough to make flowering practical and pretty? If the older limbs appear to be crowding the new ones, you should trim out the older shoots. Take out a few of the senior citizens at a time, though, or your shrubs will look skimpy.

Sharpen Up the Tools

Improper pruning equipment has killed hundreds of shrubs. Your shears must be sharp enough to swiftly and neatly trim off a branch or twig. No matter which type of shears you own, they won't do you any good if they're not sharpened. The best time to sharpen them is right after you're through pruning.

For most flowering shrubs, the long-handled, long-blade shears are best. You'll probably need a small hand pair too.

The most common mistake of amateur shrub pruners is cutting back all the top branches to the same height. No suckers or weak branches are removed.

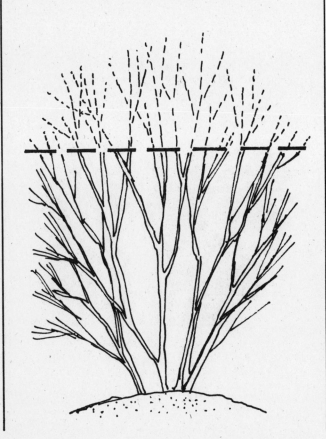

The result of such pruning is a badly shaped shrub with bare lower branches. The natural shape of the shrub is destroyed, and bloom production is severely reduced.

A Beauty Treatment

Sometimes shrubs have to be trimmed here and there for beauty purposes. With the right know-how, you can make your shrubs the most attractive on the block.

Shrubs, like everything else, tend to grow up to be what they're meant to be. You can shorten a cocker spaniel's tail, give him little pointed ears and shear off a lot of hair, but that won't make him a bull dog. Likewise, no amount of pruning is going to make a crape-myrtle a privet hedge. Shape the crape-myrtle to point out its own lovely lines; don't try to cut it down to the ground every time it reaches for the sky.

Some shrubs, like spicebushes, sweet shrubs and Chinese redbuds, look better when left alone. There is seldom a reason to prune these self-sufficient beauties as they seem to thrive on neglect as far as pruning is concerned. Sometimes these shrubs have limbs broken by ice or wind—or two-footed creatures. You need to prune, then, for repair.

Illustrated below is an example of formal pruning, which takes a lot of time and effort and is not really suited to most modern landscapes.

The purpose of more natural pruning, as illustrated below, is to emphasize the natural shape and beauty of the shrub. Over-long, weak or diseased branches were cut back.

FORMAL

INFORMAL

If a shrub freezes back, but is not killed, you should cut it back to within 3 inches of the ground. If you don't, it will look like the shrub below.

A Shapely Hedge

Hedge pruning has two sides to it. You can grow a formal hedge that must be cut regularly and kept in a definite shape, or you can grow a hedge that does what comes naturally.

As soon as you plant a deciduous hedge, you should cut it back almost to the ground. Let it grow until the next season, then begin to shape it. Always trim hedges so they're narrower at the top than at the bottom. If you reverse this, making the hedge wider at the top, the bottom branches will be shaded and will lose their leaves.

*When formally pruning your hedge,
always make the top narrower
than the bottom. If you invert
your trim, the top branches will
shade the bottom ones and cause
them to drop their leaves.*

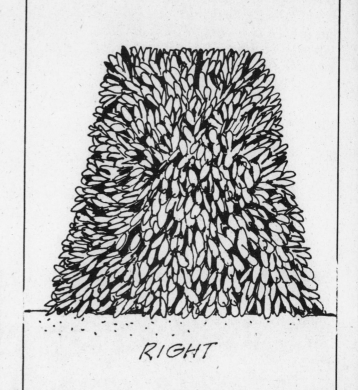

RIGHT

You might want a hedge beside a fence for beauty as well as support. Winter honeysuckle would be a beautiful and fragrant choice. It's hardy and is semi-evergreen in habit. You'll need to prune these shrubs only to remove dead wood.

Some of the most beautiful flowering hedges on earth are made of forsythia, one of the first shrubs to bloom in spring. Right behind her is the spiraea, which is equally fine as a shrub hedge. Both need only a little shaping up every now and then. Each individual bush should be allowed to grow naturally.

If you want thorny hedges, many are available and most require little pruning. Flowering quince, Japanese barberry, and Rosa rugosa are all popular. You can expect the Rosa rugosa to grow about 6 feet tall. You'll need to prune it some to keep it from becoming unsightly and to stimulate new growth. Its red hips are an excellent source of vitamin C.

Flowering quince will tolerate very little cutting, so don't annoy it with your shears. Trim the plant only if it becomes a real eyesore.

The deciduous firethorn (Pyracantha) grows from 6 to 10 feet tall. It needs pruning to cause heavier berry growth. Cut back the wood that bears fruit in the winter and pinch back new growth in the summer.

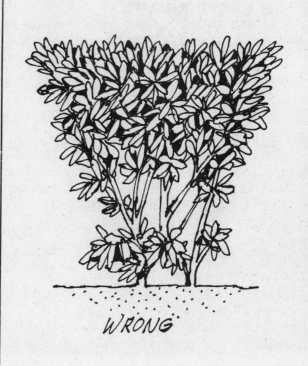

WRONG

Culture

What lovely shrubs you have, Grandma! Now I wonder how you're going to take care of them. Soil preparation and proper planting isn't enough. Flowering shrubs need to know they'll be taken care of for the rest of their lives. Being a parent is not just birthing a child; it's taking care of him through feverish nights, watching him grow that first tooth, and playing touch football on the front lawn.

Being a good flower parent means tenderly planting a flowering shrub, then watering it, mulching it, fertilizing it and cutting its blossoms when needed. Taking care of your shrub is your job from the day you say, "I do," when the nurseryman asks, "Will you take Frances Forsythia to be your own shrub until the day one of you goes to that great flower garden in the sky?"

Don't Wait for a Rainy Day

At first thought, watering may sound like the easiest step in caring for your plants. Leave it to the rain, you say, but it just isn't that easy. Some areas go for long periods with no rain at all, and other places seldom see the sunshine. How you water and the amount you give your plants can determine their future.

Watering your shrubs by sprinkling them lightly is like sprinkling your car and saying it's been washed. Sprinkling your shrubs can actually ruin them by causing the low-down feeder roots to reach upward for water. They'll weaken the shrubs when they move closer to the surface to live.

You also need the right kind of water. The best is rainwater, but Mother Nature's right-hand man, Jupiter Fluvius, doesn't always cooperate with us, so we have to use the best substitutes available.

There are many different kinds of water, and H_2O is the basic scientific formula for all kinds. Every time any moisture—rain, snow, dew—falls, it picks up natural trace elements on the way. Nitrogen is one element added during an electrical storm. The raindrops might be charged with up to 78 percent nitrogen!

Most of us have to water our shrubs with tap water with all its chemical additives, such as fluoride for teeth and chlorine for purification. Unfortunately, tap water has sodium salt additives and salt is terrible for your shrubs and lawns.

Are Your Shrubs Heavy Drinkers?

Years ago, a new Mama was told to feed her new baby every four hours on the dot. Hospital nursery attendants woke the babies up for every feeding whether they were hungry or not. Nowadays, babies are fed on the demand schedule. If they sound like they're hungry, Mama feeds them.

Gardeners' views fluctuate, too. Some believe in watering shrubs every time they look thirsty. Others believe in watering them once a week, whether they ask for it or not.

To determine how much water your flowering shrubs need, you have to consider where you live, what your soil is like, and what kind of shrubs you are growing. During a drought, you need to give your shrubs at least 2 inches of water, and you have to water in a way that will get the water to the roots.

During your shrubs' first year, you can cut back, giving them water only when they appear thirsty or during droughts.

Always water shrubs deeply. Sprinkling the surface, as this man is doing, causes the development of a shallow root system.

The Way to Water

There is a right time and a wrong time to water. I believe the best time to water shrubs is just after the sun comes up. I know that's demanding a lot, but nothing is too good for your shrubs. So water them while the dew is still on the lawn and the shrubs are still sleepy-eyed.

Always water deeply enough so the roots won't reach up for the water. Shallow roots mean dead plants. Healthy shrubs have deep, long-reaching roots, and a good water supply is essential for healthy roots.

If you water at night, you may give your shrubs a bad cold—or even pneumonia. Water early enough in the day to allow your shrubs' feet to dry out by night. You don't want to put them to bed with wet feet, do you?

Shrub-a-Dub-Dub

Every now and then I give my shrubs a bath as well as a drink. It gets rid of soot and soil and helps remove insects. Add a little biodegradable soap to the water, too. Your shrubs will appreciate it, but bugs will hate the taste of it.

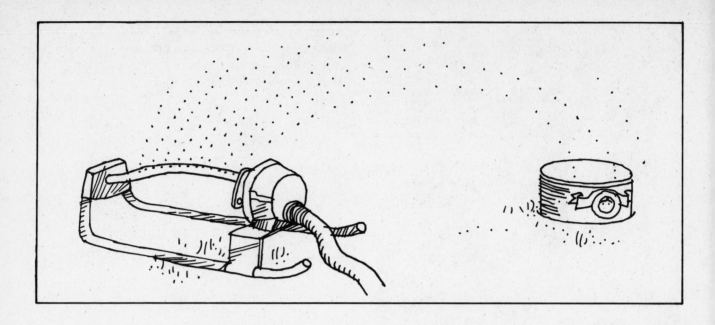

Handy Dandy Rainmakers

Basically, there are 3 ways to water when Jupiter Fluvius doesn't come through. You can use a sprinkler, a soaker or a garden hose.

If you buy a sprinkler, choose one with a large-diameter hose. Diameter determines the number of gallons the hose will put out in an hour.

One of the best automatic sprinklers on the market is equipped with both a water meter and timer. It comes on at a time decided by you, waters at a given pressure and for a prescribed length of time, then shuts off. You can stay in bed, go golfing, or do whatever you like while this sprinkler does your work. You can also buy a separate timer that shuts off the water at a set time. It costs about $10, that's well spent because it means you can turn your sprinkler on, then go back to bed without worrying about shutting it off.

You can buy a sprinkler-soaker combi-

To find out how much water a sprinkler is putting out, set a large can at the outer edge of the watering diameter. An inch of water in the can means that an inch of water has fallen on the soil.

nation hose for less than $5 per fifty feet. It acts as a sprinkler when the water pressure is high and as a soaker when the pressure is low.

You can easily tell how much water your sprinkler is putting out. Save a coffee can or large fruit can and put it at the outer edge of your watering diameter. When the can contains as much water as your shrubs need, you can shut off the sprinkler.

Go Soak Your Shrubs

A bubbler nozzle lets water flow through the hose pipe at full pressure, but the pressure is abrubtly regulated by the soaker nozzle at the end which costs about $2. Water bubbles out on top of the ground and soaks in slowly so that the soil isn't disturbed by a huge volume of water.

Some soaker hoses have tiny holes in them; others have minute slits. Both work well and will soak your soil sufficiently.

How can you tell if you're soaked long enough? Scoop up a handful of soil from about 3 inches down. If you can shape the soil into a tight ball, chances are your ground is wet all the way to the roots. If the soil is not wet enough to stick together, you need more water.

Do not under any circumstances use a high-pressure sweeper nozzle to water plants. They're great for cleaning driveways and walks, but not for soaking the roots of flowering shrubs.

I'd recommend a hose made of nylon cord with a double reinforcement. That's the material found in many modern tires which makes them last longer. Also look for kink-free non-twist hoses with brass couplings.

A reel for holding your hose pipe costs about $15, but it will prolong the life of your hose. A hose reel that can be rolled from one area of the garden to another costs a little more—about $20—but it can be a real step-saver.

Why Mulch?

Mulching is probably misunderstood more often than wives. You need to know why you're mulching, what to mulch with and when to mulch. You need to know how mulching is going to affect your flowering shrubs. Exactly why are you going to mulch that azalea?

You need to consider what your mulch job will look like. One man hauled in corncobs from everywhere to put under his shrubs. His only mistake was that he forgot to grind them up. He was the laughing stock of his neighborhood with corncobs piled a foot high under his bushes. People thought he was celebrating Halloween early. There are mulches which will make your shrubs more beautiful.

You'll need to consider the cost of mulching, too. If you're on good terms with your neighbors, I see no reason why you have to buy mulch material. Oak, maple, and elm leaves make good mulches, and using them makes good ecological sense. Burning them causes more air pollution.

When you mulch, you're helping Mother Nature. In the forest, mulching is a natural process. If you have a shaded area in your back lot, you'll see Mother Nature at work, making a lovely blanket from the leaves that fall.

One of the best reasons for mulching is to supply your soil with humus, which is the substance formed by the decomposition of organic matter. Humus holds water in your soil and contains essential plant food.

Defrosting Your Shrub

A good mulch acts as an insulator and prevents your shrubs from being affected by temperature changes. Sudden frosting and defrosting cause soil heaving which can destroy root systems. A mulch keeps this cracking from taking place.

Mulching is a must for the lazy gardener. I don't like weeding any more than you do, but I do want what's best for my plants. Mulching will cover those weeds, not just to keep your neighbors from seeing them, but to keep them from getting a start in your yard. Once in a while a determined weed might poke through the mulch, but you can easily snatch it out.

Mulching also takes care of a lot of cultivation problems by keeping the soil surface from becoming crusty. It also keeps the sun and wind from drying out the soil. If you carefully push a little mulch away from your shrubs on the hottest, driest day of the year, you'll feel cool, damp soil. So if you think you're in for a long, hot summer, you'd better mulch as soon as possible.

It's important to choose good mulch friends for your flowering children, too, because some mulches are thieves. That's right, common robbers, and I wouldn't have them associating with my shrubs for any amount of money. I've seen fresh grass clippings, wood chips, pine needles and sawdust literally steal the nitrogen from my shrubs' homes. These

materials should not be used as mulches until they have dried out and partially decomposed.

Mulches from diseased trees or lawns are no-no's too. You're kissing your shrubs good-bye if you mulch them with leaves or chips that you gathered from trees showing signs of disease. I stay away from mulches made of cocoa bean shells, buckwheat hulls and straw because they make cozy homes for mice, who are very fond of nibbling the bark of shrubs. I also dislike tobacco stems because they sometimes carry tobacco mosaic, a virus which attacks vine crops.

Did You Ever See Pine Bark?

My favorite mulches are hardwood chips, redwood and pine bark. You can also use dried-out grass clippings, leaves from disease-free trees, pebbles and wood chips.

There are now many excellent and attractive mulching materials on the market.

Use oak leaves, peat moss, and pine needles only around shrubs that require acid soil. Lime-craving shrubs will benefit from maple leaf mulches.

I don't like fine sawdust, as it mats up under shrubs and damages the root system, but coarse, partially rotted sawdust is fine. You can get it cheaply (or maybe free) from a sawmill. Ground corncobs, available at any poultry plant, are also good.

Two inches of any firm mulching material, such as wood chips, is sufficient, but 3 or 4 inches of loose material, such as leaves, is necessary. No shrub wants to be smothered, so don't pile on a thick blanket of mulch.

Nobody Loves a Fat Shrub

Fat, overfed shrubs are the mark of an amateur gardener. Fertilizer accomplishes its purpose only if it's applied properly. Too much or too little does more harm than good. Shrubs that are pruned regularly can stand a greater amount of fertilizer than the self-sufficient ones, because any overgrowth

can be taken care of with one whack of the shears.

What are the signs that your plants are hungry? Take a good look at your flowering shrubs and see how vigorously they are growing. If they're looking pale and growing poorly, they very probably need some food to perk them up.

What's for Dessert?

What kind of fertilizer do you need for your flowering shrubs? Basically, I stick with 4-12-4 and 5-10-5 garden food. My busy flowering children can gobble that right down without getting indigestion. I also reward them with occasional desserts of fish emulsion—liquid ones sometimes and dry ones other times.

Your plants have to have enough nitrogen or the foliage will be weak; enough phosphate or the feeder roots won't develop; and enough potash or the stems will be dwarfed and the flowers won't develop properly. They also need some iron, perhaps once a season.

Does it matter how you apply your fertilizer? Absolutely! I'll jump right in and say that I don't care for foliage feeding at all. You need to get to the root of the matter in fertilizing your flowering shrubs. So you need to know how to apply fertilizer to the roots. I don't ever put any plant food into the hole when I plant my flowering shrubs. I wait a couple of weeks until I know for sure that they're adjusted to their new home. Then, I'm ready to feed them.

I simply sprinkle plant food over the top of my wood-chip mulch. This doesn't tear up the mulching and it soon soaks into the soil.

If you want to get the fertilizer to the roots fast, take a crowbar or similar instrument and punch holes all around the weep line of the shrubs, making the holes about a foot apart and a foot deep. Drop a handful of 4-12-4, 5-10-5 or fish emulsion into each hole and refill it. Then water the shrub to wash the food down.

There are many fertilizers specifically blended for shrubs and trees. Ask your nurseryman to recommend a good one.

Regular Meals

From February to August, I give my small shrubs half a pound of 4-12-4 or 5-10-5 per month. My larger shrubs, about 3 to 6 feet in height, get a little more—1½ pounds. Naturally, the tallest ones, 6 feet and over, get 2½ to 3 pounds of plant food. Those hungry little rascals will love you for giving them regular meals every month.

Andy Azalea Has an Acid Tongue

Some shrubs, such as rhododendrons and azaleas, must have an acid soil and cannot live where the alkaline content is high, nor where it is hot and dry. These picky plants insist on a peaty soil with a pH value as high as 5.5 and preferably not any lower than 4.5. They love organic foods—dead wood decomposing around their feet, old roots and leaf mold.

If you plant these acid-soil shrubs in neutral or alkaline soils, you'll have to supply the acid which isn't there. The best way to do this is with acid mulches. The best mulch is peat moss because it will add acid, humus, and organic matter, all rolled up into a bale or bag. Leaf mold is also excellent. If your pH reads more than 5, you need a lot of acid, so add at least 50 percent peat moss or leaf mold to your soil.

Rotted oak leaves make good acid mulches, too, as well as pine needles. You can leave these mulches on all year round. Some people use old hops for acid plants, too. The English swear by this method.

You can use up to a foot of mulch through the winter if the weather is cold. The mulch will settle down during the winter, but if it doesn't you can remove some when you do your spring cleaning.

The Acid Test

There are two ways you can test the acidity of your soil. You can send it to a state extension laboratory and have it tested for a small fee or you can be a do-it-yourselfer. Soil-testing kits are available at any garden center.

First a soil sample must be taken, preferably with an auger. Always take several samples from various parts of the yard. Be sure that the container in which you put your soil sample hasn't held fertilizer or some other organic matter or the results of the test won't be valid.

A Heap of Fun

Compost is a mixture of decayed vegetable matter, often combined with animal manures. Compost is one of the most important means of fertilization and is an excellent soil conditioner. At planting time, it's good for replacing the soil taken from planting holes.

Making a compost heap can be as simple or as complicated as you want to make it. You can construct a block or brick bin without even mortaring them together. You can make a slat-framed bin of 2"x2" slats or a picket-fence bin. You can even make compost in a garbage can with the bottom removed.

Whatever type of compost heap you make, the top should be concave so water will collect and seep down into it.

But just what should go into your compost heap? Almost any biodegradable material. You can use kitchen scraps, straw, grass clippings and many other things. Avoid meat scraps—they smell and attract flies.

Building your heap in layers speeds up decomposition. Start with a layer of grass clippings, leaves, straw or similar material. Add a layer of stable manure, sewage sludge, bone meal, or blood meal. Then you can add some rich soil, although this is not essential. Next, add ground limestone phosphate rock or gypsum.

Of course, you don't have to be "scientific" about composting. You can just pile up whatever you have on hand or can scavenge, and it will eventually turn into fine, rich compost if you follow the basic rules of composting. It's important that the compost get plenty of ventilation, so you'll need to either turn it occasionally or drive a stake or pipe into the center of the heap. If you don't get much rain where you live, water your heap occasionally. You should let your heap alone for 6 to 12 months to allow your compost to season thoroughly.

Pests

Flowering shrubs are deceptively tough. Most of them are willing and able to defend themselves against the most insistent insect and the most disastrous disease. But if you're the gardener I hope you are, you'll give your shrubs a hand in their battle. And the best way to help them is to keep them healthy. Also remember to keep the area around them free of debris which could harbor insects or diseases. As I've already told you, prune out any infected or insect-damaged branches.

Remember that birds are truly your shrubs' fine, feathered friends, and make them feel welcome in your yard. They'll thank you by gobbling up thousands of insects and filling your life with song.

If you do see a few insects on one of your favorite shrubs, don't panic and immediately drench them with a super-toxic insecticide. If there are very few insects, just pick them off by hand and squash them. If there are too many to hand pick, try blasting them off with a hand jet of water. Check again in 2 or 3 days to see if any more insects have hatched out. If they have, blast them.

If all else fails, you can always turn to one of the various insecticides. Be sure, however, to follow the instructions on the label exactly, and store all equipment and insecticides out of the reach of children and pets.

The chart below should help you identify your insect enemies—and that's half the battle.

CATERPILLARS

Several varieties of this pest may attack your shrubs. Most commonly seen are the inchworm, or cankerworm, and the gypsy moth's larvae. The eastern tent caterpillar (illustrated) can be a real problem especially in the spring when they hatch out and hungrily devour leaves. Their familiar, webby nests in the crotches of branches may be your first signal of trouble to come.

In early spring you should apply dormant oil spray to smother the eggs of caterpillars that deposit them on twigs or in the bark. In the caterpillar stage, these pests can be controlled with Malathion or diazinon applied to the foliage in the spring and again in the summer.

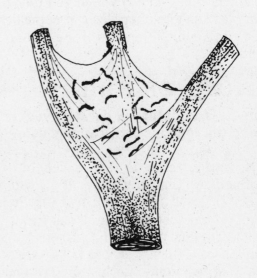

MEALY BUGS

Mealy bugs are tiny, ¼-inch scale insects, often found in small groups or colonies. They are oval and have a grayish-white appearance. Their presence is made obvious by their cottony egg masses. Malathion is very effective against these pests.

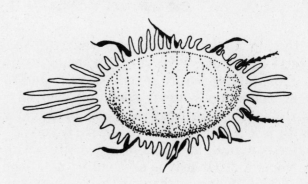

RED SPIDER MITES

These very tiny members of the spider family are serious plant pests. They cause damage by sucking the plant's juices, thereby stunting growth and discoloring leaves. Close inspection will show their fine webbing on the undersides of the leaves. Strong, frequent sprays of water will get rid of mites, but a heavy infestation probably will require a miticide such as dicofol or chlorobenzilate, used repeatedly.

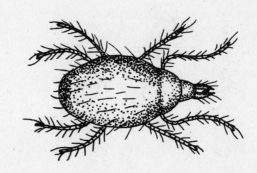

SCALE

Scales are almost invisible and they attach so closely as to appear to be part of the plant. They are very prolific. Adult males develop wings but the females settle in one place and suck the plant's sap through a long, flexible beak. Shrubs attacked by these pests turn yellow, lose leaves and may die.

Standard control includes using a dormant oil spray or lime-sulphur in early spring. Malathion or diazinon may be used in late spring or summer. Badly infested branches should be pruned out.

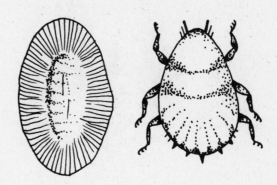

Propagation

Buying all the shrubs you want can get pretty expensive if you're a real shrub lover. Fortunately, there are several ways to add to your collection without spending a penny. Most shrubs are very easy to propagate. With just a little effort on your part, you can have as many duplicates of a favorite shrub as you want. Or maybe a friend or neighbor would be willing to share with you. You can grow your own shrubs from divisions, from softwood or hardwood cuttings, by layering, from root cuttings or from seeds. Your choice will depend on the season of the year, the number of plants you need and your own preference.

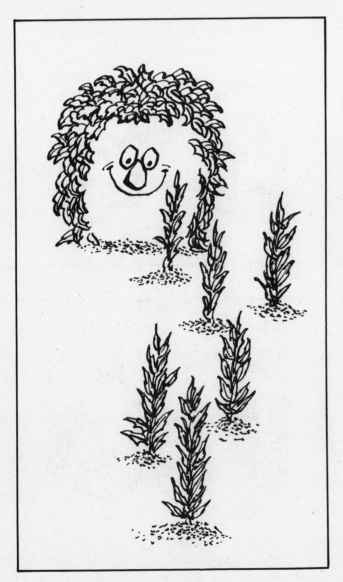

1. Softwood cuttings can be taken in late spring or summer. Using a sharp knife, cut at an angle to remove a 5-7 inch healthy stem tip.

2. Remove flowers, buds or leaves on the lower third of the stem. To aid your chances of success, dip about ½ inch of the stem end in rooting hormone.

3. Moisten your rooting material [equal parts of sand and peat moss is a good mixture] and set the stems about 2 inches deep and 3 inches apart. Water again. Make a small "greenhouse" by covering the container with plastic, tucked in around the edges.

"I'm so proud! All my cuttings look just like me."

Softwood Cuttings

1

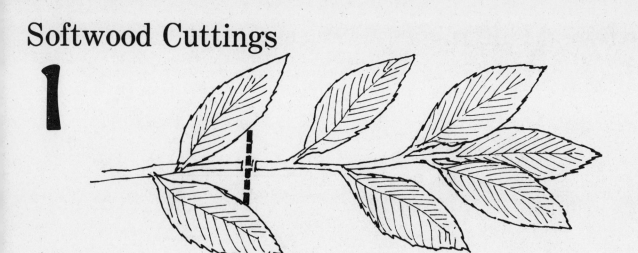

2   **3**

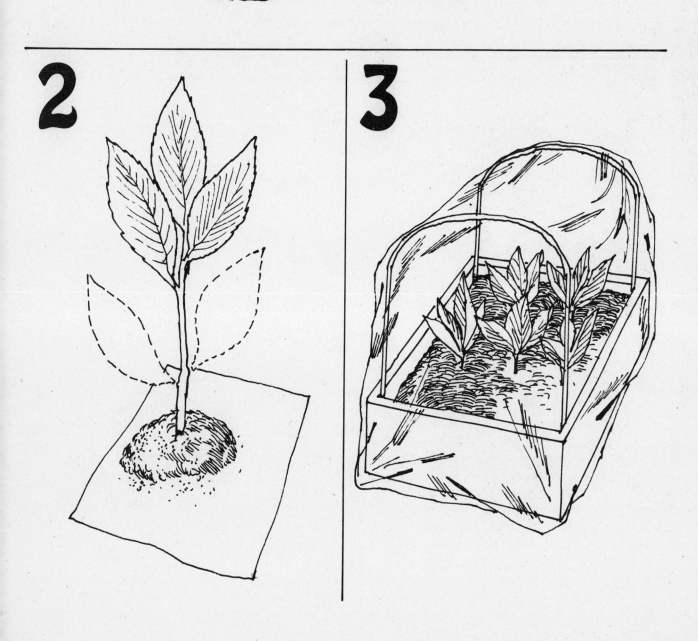

Hardwood Cuttings

1

In late fall or early winter, take cuttings [6 to 8 inches long] of current season's growth, using either canes that grow from the plant's base, or new growth on ends of branches.

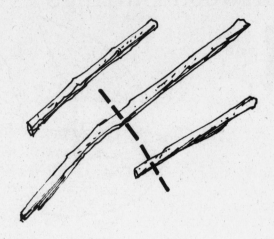

2

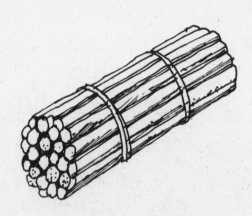

Gather and tie cuttings into bundles of convenient size, with all tops at the same end; label this end, "top."

3

Bury the bundle in a mixture such as sand and peat moss. During the first 3 or 4 weeks of storage, the temperature should be 50-55 degrees F. After that the temperature should be kept at 35 to 40 degrees until spring. In early spring, plant the cuttings 4 to 6 inches apart. The following year you should prune back almost to the ground. Cuttings are ready for permanent homes that fall or the next spring.

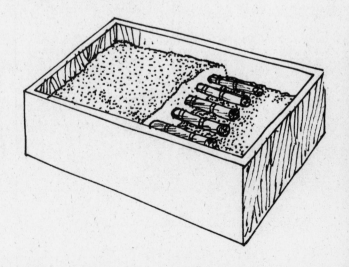

Root Cuttings

1

Root cuttings should be made in early spring or late fall. With a sharp spade, drive into the ground about one-third of the way in from the spread of the outermost branches.

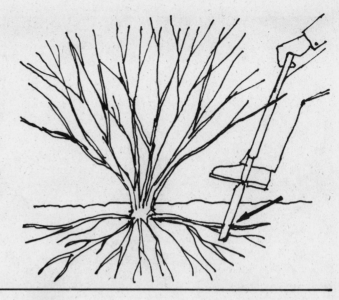

2

Remove the cut root sections of the spreading roots by spading down again about 18 inches further out. Use 2-3 inch portions of these, burying each into a nursery bed hole about 3 inches deep, 4 inches wide on a layer of damp peat moss. Cover with soil and firm soil with your foot.

3

New roots will form along the length of the cutting and a young plant will appear in a few months. The next year you may plant the baby shrub in its permanent location.

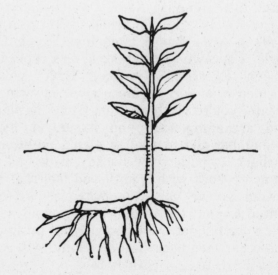

Landscaping

A lot of people have the wrong impression of landscaping. They think landscaping is an art practiced only by experienced professionals—for very wealthy clients. And they are only partially wrong—having your lawn landscaped is definitely not cheap. But, believe it or not, you can do a professional-quality landscaping job yourself. All it takes is a little know-how, a little taste and a lot of planning.

First of all you need to know what you want to accomplish with your landscaping. Do you want a formal scene or an informal look? Is your house a compact Cape Cod style, a sprawling ranch style or a replica of Queen Elizabeth's palace? Once you've decided what sort of impression you want to create, you're ready to start choosing plants and arranging them—on paper, at least. Remember the paper-bag plan I mentioned earlier? If you haven't already made one, do so now. Work with it until you feel that the design you've come up with is perfectly suited to your lot, your house, your lifestyle and your budget. Now submit your design to the other members of your family. After all, they have to live with it too.

The Natural Look Is In

With everyone's thoughts turning to ecology, we're all wanting to go back to the natural look. And flowering shrubs are happiest when they're allowed to follow their natural instincts. If you have enough room, a naturalized shrub planting will give your landscape a casual, woodsy look, and it will be very easy to maintain. I especially like naturalized plantings on hillsides and in woodlands.

A naturalized planting should look as if Mother Nature planted it for you. I always think of rhododendrons when I think of naturalizing because I first saw these plants in the Smoky Mountains. Whenever I see a pink rhododendron I want to retrace that scenic route. The vase-shaped spice bush is another good candidate for naturalizing, as are dogwoods, witch hazels and elderberries. High-bush blueberries produce delicate flowers, scarlet autumn foliage, and delicious fruit.

Winning Combinations

The combination of shrubs, evergreens and flowering plants are so numerous that a computer would blow a fuse trying to figure them out. Many of the dogwood species have colored bark which is pretty in winter especially when seen against a background of evergreens. The less attractive winter shrubs, such as the deciduous mock-orange and butterfly bush, are good to plant behind low-growing evergreens which will provide contrast in summer and camouflage in winter.

Flowering quince, barberry, privet, honeysuckle and many others help feed your bird friends during the winter months and brighten up the landscape at a time when most plants are barren. Their berries perk up you and your fine, feathered friends.

Think about what your barks look like together and whether or not one area of your yard will be heavy with foliage when another area is sparse. You can plant your entire yard so that it is balanced all year long.

Give Yourself a Break

Are you tired of looking at your neighbors' garbage cans? Or are you afraid that old north wind is going to huff and puff and blow your house down? In either case, a flowering shrub fence is just what you need. Of course, you could use evergreens, but they look the same all year long. Flowering shrubs change from season to season, offering blossoms, autumn color and often fruit or berries.

You can prune flowering fences, but I prefer the natural look myself. Deutzia, euonymus, forsythia, privet, pomegranate, spiraea, lilac, snowball and cranberry are some of the best choices for an untrimmed hedge. If you choose shrubs of approximately the same height, you can plant several different shrubs in the same hedge, and they need not all bloom at the same time.

Guide to Shrubs

Azalea (Rhododendron)

Azaleas are capable of yielding an extra-ordinary harvest of beauty, but they do not offer this freely. It must be earned. But to those who fall in love with this lovely flower, no effort is too much.

So that there will be no confusion, let me say that botanists now classify all azaleas as rhododendrons. Under this name are now included not only the evergreen kinds which have large, leathery leaves, but also the deciduous or leaf-losing varieties.

Azaleas, which flower in spring or early summer, may grow only 18 inches tall or attain a height of 15 feet or more.

The soil for azaleas should resemble, as nearly as possible, that in which they grow naturally—a cushion of acid leaf mold. It should have a large content (60 to 90 percent) of organic matter. This may be leaf mold, peat moss, humus or decomposed pine, hemlock or spruce needles, or a mixture of any of these. Good quality soil and a little sand should make up the rest.

Azaleas are "surface-rooters," but you should give them at least 18 inches of this compost and a good mulch of partially de-cayed leaves so their roots will remain cool and moist during the hot summer months. They should also have mulch in winter as a protection against severe cold. Most azaleas grow naturally in light, open woodlands or on the fringes of the woods. If shade is too heavy or too continuous, they will not flower freely. On the other hand, they do not like the scorching heat of summer and they insist on having their roots cool and moist. Place them where they will receive some shade or in an area to the north or northeast of the house where they will receive some sunlight for part of the day but shade the rest of the time.

Azalea

Since azaleas have many feeding roots close to the surface, mulching is preferable to cultivation for keeping down weeds.

Some azaleas will not tolerate extremes of cold and others will resent prolonged summer heat, particularly in areas where there is no dependable period of winter chilling, for all azaleas require some winter rest.

Hardy azaleas may be raised from seeds sown in pots or shallow flats. Sow them in February, March or April in sandy, peaty soil, and place them in a slightly heated greenhouse or coldframe. The best insurance against damping off is to sow the seeds in sphagnum moss. Fill the flats or pots with good soil and cover it with a ½-inch layer of moss which has been rubbed through a ¼-inch mesh or sieve.

For cuttings, choose half-ripe or semi-woody shoots of the current year's growth. Make these 2 or 3 inches long and take them off with a very thin heel or piece of the old branch during July. Place in the greenhouse in a mixture of sand and peat moss. Keep the frame closed for 3 or 4 weeks to encourage the cuttings to form roots, watering them after insertion and keeping them moist by daily spraying if necessary.

You may also increase your stock by layering the lower branches in the summer.

Barberry (Berberis)

There are many good reasons for growing barberries. Some are famous for their beautiful and fragrant flowers, others become outstandingly attractive when covered with bright-colored fruits later in the year. They are adaptable to many types of soil, easily transplanted, and tolerant of light shade. They will, however, have more brilliant autumn color if grown in full sun.

Barberries will thrive in a wide range of soils from sandy loam to clayey loam. The evergreen types are best planted in spring; the leaf-losing types may be either fall or spring planted. This shrub will grow into a well-shaped bush naturally, so pruning is rarely necessary. If cutting back does become necessary, do this as soon as the flowering period is over. Barberries make excellent hedge plants, generally requiring only one annual clipping.

You may increase your supply by sowing seeds as soon as they have ripened or in early spring. Put them in a coldframe in flats or pots filled with two parts good garden loam, one part leaf mold and one part sand. Prick

Barberry

out the young plants and pot singly in small pots when they are large enough to handle. Later they may be transferred to the nursery border.

All barberries may be increased by cuttings. Take short shoots 3 or 4 inches long in July or August and place them in a bed of sand or a mixture of sand and peat moss, preferably in a coldframe. Cuttings take about 6 months to become sufficiently rooted for transplanting.

Occasionally suckers are detached from large plants to form new bushes.

The evergreen barberries, which retain their leaves through the winter, are exceedingly handsome. One of the hardiest of these is Berberis Julianae, which comes from China.

Among the red-fruited barberries, B. Wilsonae is a dense shrub about 3 feet high with very spiny branches. Its small leaves fall in winter and its main attraction is the coral red fruit it bears in autumn. The berries are bundled rather than clustered, and are preceded by yellow flowers. The ripe fruits will yield a good jelly. A choice brandy is also made from the berries, and special, large-fruited types have been developed for this use. The soft, inner bark of the barberries is said to have a healing effect if rubbed on chapped hands or lips.

Beach Plum (Prunus maritima)

This native shrub of our eastern coast is a spreading bush which may be trained into a small tree. It occurs naturally near the coast from New Brunswick to Virginia. Its height is variable, ranging from 4 to 10 feet. It is exceedingly attractive in bloom and produces edible fruit which may be either dull purple or yellow. It is best used for naturalistic plantings.

Beauty Bush (Kolkwitzia amabilis)

Beauty bush is a leaf-losing shrub that comes to us from China and belongs to the honeysuckle family. The flowers of beauty bush are borne in great profusion in early June and, though smaller and far more abundant, greatly resemble weigelas. The bell-shaped flowers are a lovely pink with a golden throat. They contrast beautifully with the soft, gray-green foliage which remains on the bush into autumn.

Beauty bush is a vigorous shrub growing 8 to 9 feet tall, but it may be pruned back to a lower height if desired. It is also characterized by a bark which peels away from the stems in large flakes.

This shrub is perfectly hardy and will thrive in any fair, well-drained garden soil in full sun or very light shade. It may be pro- pagated by either cuttings or seeds, but cuttings are preferable because seedlings show great variations both in color and flower size.

Since beauty bush will grow quite tall as it matures, it is advisable to place it in the background of the border.

Beauty Bush

Blueberry (Vaccinium corymbosum)

This is the "high-bush" blueberry and it is very ornamental because of the brilliant orange-red to scarlet color of its autumn foliage. Sometimes called the swamp blueberry, it is a leaf-losing shrub which may grow as tall as 12 feet but is usually much shorter. Native to eastern North America, it is very insistent upon having an acid, peaty soil and requires for its best development abundant moisture at its roots.

It has white, pink-touched flowers, cylindrical in shape, which appear in small clusters in May. They are followed by nearly black fruits. Large-fruited kinds combine beauty with usefulness. This shrub has great value for large-scale, naturalistic plantings, but grows rather large for an average lot.

Pruning should be done in late fall, winter or early spring. Up to the age of about 3 years, the bushes will need comparatively little pruning. Simply remove the small, weak, lateral twigs to prevent their fruiting. The long shoots, well covered with fruit buds, may need cutting back so that only 2 or 3 fruit buds remain. Remember that one fruit bud will produce a cluster of flowers, usually followed by a cluster of fruit. If not thinned, too many small, late-maturing berries will be set, and this will weaken the bush.

The best time to make blueberry cuttings is in late winter or early spring. Cut 6-inch hard-wood cuttings from one-year-old twigs, preferably without fruit buds. Place them at an angle in a mixture of peat moss and sand, covering at least 2/3 of the cutting. Use great care in watering and ventilating.

Bottle-brush Buckeye (Aesculus parviflora)

Bottle-brush buckeye, which grows only 7 to 10 feet tall, is at home in small gardens and is excellent for use as a lawn specimen. The erect, foot-long, candle-like spires of white blossoms produce a striking effect in July and August. Coming at a time when few other things are in bloom, the flowers are particularly welcome.

Buckeye forms a large, billowy shrub and increases in width by means of suckering roots. Left to itself, it will in time form a large patch.

The leaves are 5- to 7-fingered. They are somewhat coarse and plain, but turn an attractive yellow-gold in autumn, again adding color to the scene.

Buckeye is native to the southeastern United States but is reliably hardy further north. This shrub will grow readily in average soils. It is most effective in open situations but will do quite well in light shade.

Butterfly Bush (Buddleia)

These lovely, colorful, summer- and autumn-flowering shrubs are easy to grow and have great value in the home garden. Many are hardy; others are suitable for outdoor planting only in mild areas. Most are deciduous, or leaf-losing. There is considerable variation in the height, which ranges from 3 to 15 feet. The blossoms come in many exquisite colors, including deep rose-purple, white, purple, flaming violet, pale lilac and many shades in between, some of which are made even more striking by the orange eyes. A very graceful Chinese type, the weeping willow buddleia, grows 10 feet tall and bears delicate clusters of mauve flowers in June.

Most buddleias will grow in ordinary garden soil to which some organic matter has been added, preferably decayed manure. They may be planted in either spring or fall.

It is important to prune this shrub correctly. The types which flower in late summer and autumn should be pruned each spring by cutting back the shoots of the previous year's growth to within 2 or 3 inches of the older wood.

In severe climates, the bush may be killed back to the ground during the winter, but as long as the roots survive, new growth will be produced and it will bloom the same summer. Mulching the plants during the winter months will be of great benefit, particularly in climates where the ground is subject to hard freezing.

Buddleias are readily propagated by cuttings. These, which may be either half-ripe wood or semi-woody side shoots, should be 5 to 6 inches long. Place in a coldframe or outdoors in a sheltered, shady location and keep moist.

Buddleias are always happiest and most effective in a sunny location. Here they will add to the beauty of the garden by attracting large numbers of butterflies during the day and numerous moths at night.

Broom (Cytisus)

The brooms are delightful plants, bearing pea-like flowers of many colors. One of the most effective, the spike-broom, is distinguished by erect, spike-like racemes of yellow, honey-scented flowers, at their showy best in July.

Brooms, which reach a height of about 4 to 5 feet, have rather dull, gray-green, 3-fingered leaves. It is useful as a light, flowery garden hedge if placed in a sunny location. Prune back to desired height after the flowering season. Brooms do best in well-drained, rather light soils, but clay can be made more suitable by adding sand and compost.

The wild types may be propagated by seeds sown in pots or flats as soon as they have ripened. Soaking the seeds 24 hours before planting aids in germination. Varieties which do not come true from seeds should be increased by means of cuttings. Place them in a bed of sandy soil in a coldframe in August, or in a shaded spot outdoors. Make the cuttings from firm summer shoots. They should be 3 to 4 inches long and have a small piece of the older wood attached.

Brooms do not transplant very successfully, so they should be grown in pots until they are large enough for planting in their permanent location. For the first 2 or 3 years, the new shoots on the young plants should be cut back several times during the growing season to assure the formation of well-branched plants.

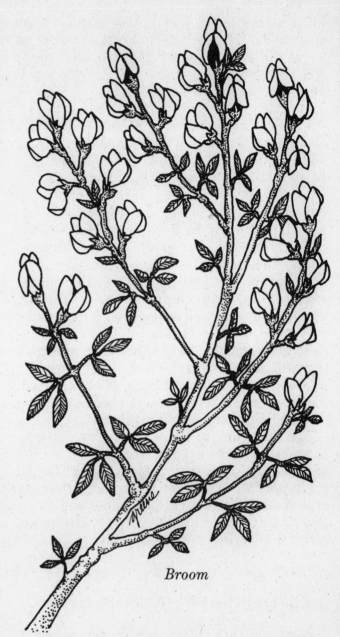

Broom

Cherry Laurel (Prunus laurocerasus)

Cherry laurel is greatly valued as a hedge shrub, as a screen plant and for shade. Left unpruned, it will form a large evergreen bush about 15 to 25 feet in height, but is most effective as a dense hedge. There are several named varieties which vary in habit of growth and size of leaves. Some have narrow leaves of a rich green and others have large, glossy leaves.

Cherry laurels are of easy culture in any reasonably fertile, well-drained soil. It will thrive in sun or shade and stands pruning well. Plant in early spring just before new growth begins, or in early fall after the season's growth is completed. The planting should be done while the soil is still warm enough to encourage the development of new roots and to enable the plant to become established before cold weather. Water should be freely given, especially for a late summer or fall planting.

Chinese Redbud (Cercis chininsis)

Chinese redbud is a very handsome plant which may be grown as a tree or tall shrub. It has attractive pea-shaped flowers and gray-green leaves. The deep pink flowers, larger than those of the native American species, are borne profusely in early spring and few leaves are apparent at the time of blooming. The leaves, though sometimes difficult to distinguish from the native species, are generally of a firmer, somewhat leathery texture and usually a deeper green. The flowers are a deeper purple, a darker, richer rose than the flowers of the American redbud.

Chinese redbud grows to a height of 50 feet in its native area, but in the region of New York it seldom grows over 3 or 4 feet tall. It is not reliably hardy, except in sheltered locations.

This shrub thrives well either in full sun or light shade and is attractive used in the foreground of the border.

Both Chinese redbud and the American species are difficult to transplant, and it is advisable to move them only in the early spring. Always be sure to keep a ball of earth around the roots.

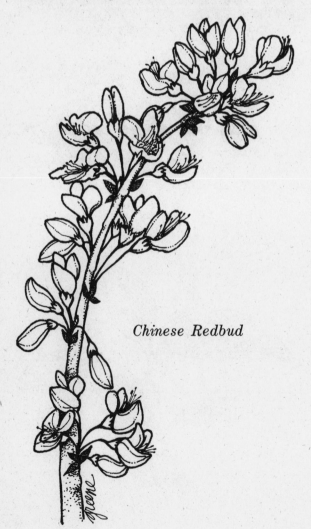

Chinese Redbud

Cotoneaster

The cotoneasters are quite a large family, and since some members are far more attractive than others, varieties should be chosen with care. Some species are hardy, but most cotoneasters are more adapatable and more beautiful if grown in the milder regions of the country.

There are both leaf-losing and evergreen cotoneasters. They are valued chiefly for their fruits, though some have attractive white flowers resembling spiraea blossoms. Generally speaking, the leaf-losing types are hardy in the North, while the evergreen types are more suitable for southern gardens.

Propagation is by seeds or cuttings. The seeds should be sown in late autumn in a cold frame or greenhouse in pots of sandy soil.

Cuttings 4 to 6 inches long are made from shoots of the current year's growth. They may be grown in the greenhouse or in a sheltered location outdoors if winters are mild.

Cotoneasters are of very easy culture, thriving in almost any kind of soil, even in poor soil where other shrubs find it difficult to become established. You will, however, be rewarded with better plants if some decayed manure or organic matter is added to the soil.

In height, the cotoneasters vary from a few inches to many feet. For this reason, their uses in the garden are many and varied, some being ideal for the shrubbery border, others for the rock garden, and still others are good specimen shrubs. Some are useful as hedges or naturalized in the open woodland.

Pruning is not a great problem, for they require very little. With the leaf-losing kinds, thin any crowded branches or shorten those that have grown too long. Do this in late fall or during the winter. The evergreen kinds should be pruned about the middle of April.

Cotoneasters may be planted in fall or spring. Small potted plants are the most succesful.

Crape Myrtle (Lagerstroemia)

Crape myrtle, the southern belle of shrubs, is one of the showiest of all. It now comes in a full range of colors, as well as in dwarf sizes that may be grown anywhere.

If "beauty is its own excuse for being," then surely this shrub needs no other. It has long been a southern favorite and is probably more widely planted than any other woody perennial. And with good reason. In regions of little summer rainfall, this stately queen will stand up and bloom when other plants falter and fail.

Standard-size crape myrtle of the older varieties will grow as tall as 25 to 30 feet. Though there are both white and light violet types, the preferred color seems to be a luscious shade of watermelon pink. And the closely packed clusters of individual flowers,

each about an inch wide, really do resemble fluffed-up crepe paper. Morever, the season of bloom usually extends from July to September when few other flowers are seen.

No shrub is easier to propagate than a crape myrtle. I have started dozens of new plants by simply inserting cuttings in the ground in the fall of the year. These cuttings, 12 to 15 inches long, should be inserted to a

Crape Myrtle

74

depth of about 6 to 8 inches in a shady location and kept fairly moist. They will root readily and may be moved to a permanent location the following spring.

Crape myrtles are by no means confined to the South. In fact, in sheltered places, specimens will survive all but the most severe winters, even as far north as New York City. Should the tops be winter killed, remove the dead wood by pruning in spring to encourage the development of new shoots that will bloom the same season. Shape for balanced growth, thinning out weak and superficial shoots. Do this before growth starts, never after.

Those who live in severe climates may still enjoy crape myrtles by using the dwarf types in tubs and boxes to brighten up a porch or outdoor area. In winter, store in a frostproof place and keep very nearly dry.

Daphne

Daphnes, both evergreen and deciduous types, are attractive dwarf shrubs, especially valued for their highly fragrant flowers. In the species Daphne Mezereum, the small, purple, spice-scented flowers cover the wood in earliest spring. It rarely grows over 3 feet tall and is of a stiffly erect habit of growth.

Daphne belongs to a large family. Some are perfectly hardy, while others are suitable for outdoor cultivation only in the South.

Propagation varies according to species, but seeds should be used if possible. Sow them as soon as they are ripe in pots or flats in a compost of loam, peat moss and sand. Some of the very fragrant kinds are best increased by cuttings which should be inserted in a warm propagation frame in early spring.

Daphnes, especially the stronger-growing ones, like deep, loamy soil and dislike hot, dry conditions. Some thrive in shade, and many of the dwarf varieties are suitable for rock gardens.

Deutzia

Deutzia

Deutzias are splendid for spring and early summer flowering, but they are otherwise undistinguished. The majority are of imperfect hardiness in most sections of the country, though easily grown in the South. If you want to grow them, be sure to give them a sheltered location and a good mulch during the winter months.

Deutzias grow about 5 feet tall on the average, but some species are as tall as 10 feet at maturity. They prefer a sunny location, but will tolerate light shade.

It is easy to increase all of the deutzuas by

means of cuttings, which should be of soft shoots, about 3 to 4 inches long. Take cuttings in May or early June. Later cuttings of firmer wood may be taken in July. Place them in the greenhouse in a bed of sandy peat. When well rooted, set the young plants in the nursery border, pinching off the ends of the shoots, so the plant will be bushy. They are usually large enough for permanent planting when about 2 years old.

If you would have plants that flower freely, encourage them to form well-ripened wood each year. Remove some of the old wood as soon as the flowering season is over. Cut back the old shoots to the point where vigorous young ones are developing. The shrub will also be benefited by an occasional application of well-rotted manure or other organic matter.

Most of the deutzias range from white through several shades of pink and rose, a few bearing purplish flowers. Some of the newer hybrids are very attractive, and most of these are in the 3- to 5-foot range.

Flowering Almond (Prunus triloba plena)

Flowering almonds grow into low bushes, though with favorable conditions they may grow as tall as 10 feet or more. They bear a profusion of pink, rosette-shaped flowers in early spring. These are borne in small clusters densely packed along the branches and appear before the development of the leaves. Among other decorative possibilities is its adaptability for espaliering against a wall. Trained in this manner, flowering almonds should be pruned each year after flowering.

Young plants are easily transplanted in the spring, even if bare-rooted. They prefer light, well-drained soil in full sun. They are grafted on wild stocks, so take care to remove all sprouts which arise from below the point where they were budded. Most small garden tragedies with flowering almonds occur because this is neglected and the wild stock takes over.

Flowering Quince

Flowering Quince (Chaenomeles)

Japanese quince has a lot going for it. One of the loveliest of early-spring-flowering shrubs, it forms a bush 10 to 12 feet high. There are a number of beautiful varieties, and you have a choice of white, pink or crimson flowers. There is even a lovely semi-double type, rose-pleno. To make things even more interesting, the pretty flowers are followed by aromatic fruits which may be used for making a delicious jelly.

Quinces may be espaliered. You may encourage flowering by pruning the side shoots in summer to about 5 leaves. Then cut back to 2 buds in winter.

I have grown flowering quince as a hedge shrub and recommend it highly. Little cutting is necessary to keep it compact, and in many situations the spiny branches are an advantage. When so grown, it will flower well in spring. Pruning should be done in early summer after the flowering season.

Flowering quince, sometimes called "japonica," belongs to the rose family. It will thrive in ordinary loamy soil and is very showy if grown in a sunny position in the open garden. Flowering quince is hardy but loses its leaves in winter, at which time the branches are still shapely and attractive.

You may easily increase your stock by layering the branches in autumn or by removing suckers which often appear around the base of established bushes. Cuttings, which may be made in summer of firm shoots, can be rooted in a compost mixture of sandy loam and peat. Seeds may also be sown in soil of this type in a greenhouse or coldframe in the spring. The named varieties will not come true to type from seeds and should be increased by cuttings.

The dwarf Japanese quince, now called Chaenomeles japonica, rarely exceeds three feet in height and produces its deep red flowers very freely in April. There are also white, pink and crimson varieties.

Forsythia

Forsythias are beautiful, hardy, leaf-losing shrubs, perhaps more commonly planted than any other. Cherished everywhere as evidence of spring's return, in March they bear a profusion of golden-yellow flowers which usually last well into April.

The upright types are very handsome in or out of flower, and have a broad, sweeping growth habit. The leaves, which soon follow the flowers, remain green until late fall.

The height varies, according to variety, the dwarfs being only 2 feet tall, others growing as tall as 10 feet.

All members of this good-natured family are easily transplanted and grow equally well

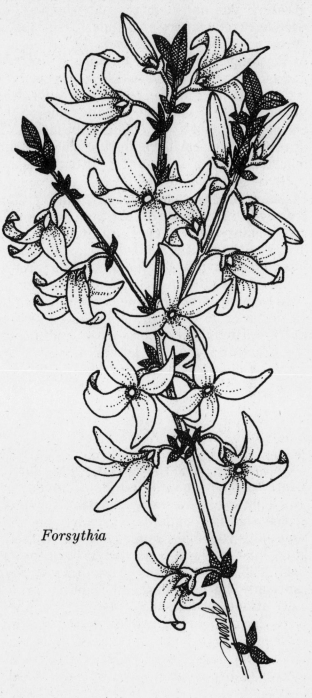

Forsythia

in sun or light shade. They are dependable bloomers, rarely injured by severe winters unless they are planted in exposed places or in low-lying frost pockets. If freezing does occur, you may get little more than token blooming that particular spring, but this is rare.

Forsythias grow easily in any good garden soil, but are more vigorous and flower more freely if you dig in some peat, compost, or well-decayed manure and mulch them well in late spring or early summer.

Planting may be done in spring, but late fall is best. Pruning should be done annually as soon as the flowering season is over. The flower buds for the next year develop on the short side shoots of the old branches. If forsythias are cut back during the dormant season, the greater part of their floral display will be sacrificed.

Forsythia may be propagated by either cuttings or layering. Soft cuttings, which will root readily, may be made in June or July. These cuttings, 3 to 4 inches long, should be inserted in a propagating case in a green-house or coldframe. Semi-woody cuttings may be made later in the season and inserted outdoors or in a coldframe. You can even make cuttings of mature wood and insert them in sandy soil as late in the year as October or November, and they will root easily.

Heath (Erica)

These are acid-soil plants for sunny locations. They may be either deciduous or evergreen; all have very beautiful flowers.

The hardy kinds are dwarf shrubs, especially valuable for gardens where there is no lime in the soil, particularly on peaty land. The tender heaths grow quite slowly, especially when young, and require careful cultivation. Because they're so finicky, they have declined in popularity in competition with more quickly grown plants.

Both the hardy and tender types can be increased by cuttings of short side shoots that are just starting to get firm. These side shoots should be only about an inch long. Remove the leaves from the lower ⅔ of the stem, taking care that the delicate bark is not torn. Insert cuttings in sandy peat which has been made firm and covered with a layer of sand. (They will take root most easily in a propagating frame.) The cuttings will take several weeks to root and should be watered carefully.

There are tree heaths from the Mediterranean region which grow 12 to 20 feet high and bear fragrant white flowers. Other tree heaths of more dwarf growth bear red or rosy-purple flowers.

Heather (Calluna)

The name "heath" is applied to the Ericas, while "heather" is reserved for Calluna. Heathers are hardy, rather small, evergreen shrubs which grow wild in many parts of Europe and in a few places in North America. The name Calluna is derived from "kallunein," meaning "to sweep," for the branches were frequently used as brooms.

Heathers look their best when grown in irregular masses, making excellent ground covers where the soil is acid and well drained. Do not try to grow them in wet, poorly drained land.

They should be planted in early fall or spring and set about a foot apart. Each spring, before new growth becomes apparent, the shoots of the previous season should be cut off close to the base of the plants.

Cuttings may be taken in July or August and placed in the greenhouse in a mixture of sand and peat moss.

Honeysuckle (Lonicera)

Japanese honeysuckle is the common half-evergreen twining shrub that has become naturalized in a large portion of the United States. Few plants give so much satisfaction for the small amount of care required. And the characteristic fragrance makes it very desirable for planting at the entrance to yards or residences. The flowers open white but change to creamy yellow.

This species may be used as a vine, as a hedge or ground cover, or even as a low bush. It may be propagated by layering or seeds.

Everblooming honeysuckle starts blooming in spring and continues throughout the growing season. The buds and outer parts of the bloom are an attractive purplish-red color, and the inner part is yellow. This honeysuckle is slow-growing and not as vigorous as the Japanese type. It may also be used as a ground cover or low hedge but will take longer to cover. Propagation is by cuttings.

A third type, trumpet honeysuckle, is native from Connecticut to Florida and Texas. It is a twining vine, and the bloom is an attractive orange scarlet on the outside and yellow on the inside. It blooms in spring and early summer with a scattering of blooms in the fall. It grows best where moisture conditions are favorable.

Hydrangea

These handsome shrubs may be either hardy or tender and even include several woody climbers. A few of the tender types are evergreen, but most are leaf-losing. When anyone thinks hydrangeas, they almost invariably picture the blue ones, though the natural pink color is just as lovely. Remember that hydrangeas which have pink flowers naturally will bear blue blossoms in districts where the soil is either acid or treated with one of the several substances which will cause the flowers to change color. White-flowered types will not turn blue but become an unattractive slate color. Deep pink flowers are the best subjects for they will become a rich and intense blue if treated with one of the chemical bluing powders sold by garden supply centers for this purpose. Other ways of changing the color include mixing iron filings in the soil, watering with alum (one teaspoonful dissolved in a gallon of water) or with 3 ounces of aluminum sulphate dissolved in a gallon of water.

Hydrangeas produce their largest flower clusters at the tips of the shoots formed the previous season. If these terminal buds are destroyed by either excessive winter cold or pruning at the wrong time, you will have little bloom. Prune in summer as soon as the flowering season is over. Remove all the old shoots which have flowered down to a point on the stem where new growth is developing.

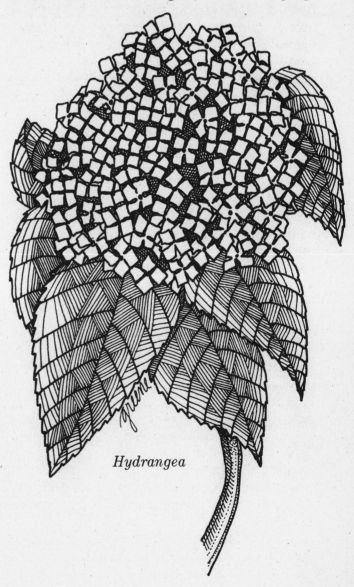

Hydrangea

Also cut out weak and crowded shoots at this time. The strong new shoots appearing at the base of the plant and on the lower parts of the old stems should be kept, for these are the shoots which may be expected to produce the next season's bloom. Never prune in late fall, winter or spring if you want flowers.

I have found that tipping a bushel basket over my hydrangea plant and then covering this with leaves affords excellent winter protection. I always uncover it as soon as the weather warms up, and I often find that it has made good growth inside the basket.

Cuttings are the easiest way of increasing your stock. Take these from the ends of the nonflowering shoots any time from April to August, being careful to retain 2 or 3 pairs of leaves on each cutting. Remove the bottom pair of leaves and cut the stem across just below a joint. Insert in a bed of sand in the greenhouse or in a coldframe. Keep closed until cuttings are well rooted, but moisten at intervals as needed.

When the cuttings are rooted, gradually admit more air, and when the young plants are hardened off a bit, pot them up separately in small pots. They should be planted in a compost of peat, leaf mold and sandy, lime-free loam. If you want pink or white hydrangeas, use fibrous loam which contains lime. Do not use loam containing lime on blue-flowered hydrangeas.

Kerria

Kerria is a lovable, multi-purpose little shrub that seldom grows more that 4 feet high. Its pretty, five-petaled flowers look somewhat like a wild rose and are at their golden best in shade, as they are apt to be rather badly bleached in full sun. They are borne on gracefully arching branches.

Kerria is very useful as an underplanting in lightly shaded locations where it will provide a pleasing, lacy pattern even in winter after it loses its leaves. The bright green, slender leaves turn a bright, clear yellow in

the fall and hold on for a long time before they drop.

Like many other obliging shrubs, Kerria will grow fairly well in ordinary garden soil but does its best if planted in ground enriched with compost or well-decomposed manure.

Kerria is not completely hardy and may freeze back in severe winter weather, but even this is, in a way, an advantage for there will be little pruning necessary in the spring. Such injury is likely to be less severe in shaded than in open locations. If your climate is not severe and pruning becomes necessary, do this immediately after the shrub has flowered, generally during the last half of May. To do this correctly, cut back the old branches to where strong new shoots are forming. Also cut any crowded, weak, or worn out branches at this time.

You can easily increase your stock by division of clumps in spring or fall.

Korean Abelialeaf (Abeliophyllum)

Abelia, judged on the merits of the foliage alone, is worthy of consideration for the home landscape. However, there is the added attraction of the fragrant, pink-tinted flowers which appear continuously from late June until late fall. These grow in small, loosely branched flower clusters along the side branches. And these are followed by brown fruits which add a further decorative touch to the little shrub.

The shoots splash out into a graceful bush about 2½ feet high and are covered with small, shiny intensely green leaves which turn a rich red touched with bronze in the fall.

Abelia has many practical uses on the home grounds. Place it wherever you need a mass of foliage to serve as an unobtrusive low filler. It may also be used as a shrub border or a low hedge.

Abelia will thrive in any good soil that has been enriched with leaf mold, compost, or peat moss. They will stand part-day shade but prefer full sun. Plant in spring or early fall.

Prune in spring by cutting out the old shoots or branches which have bloomed, along with dead branches and weak, spindly growth. Leave fresh young shoots uncut to blossom. Even if this shrub is winter killed right down to the ground (but the roots are still alive), flowers will appear on the new shoots the same year they spring from the roots.

If you would increase your stock, take cuttings, about 3 inches long, of half-ripened or semi-woody shoots of the current year's growth. Cut them in July or August and place in pots or flats of sandy soil in a propagating case or coldframe. Keep moist until roots are formed, which should take place in about 4 or 5 weeks.

Kousa or Japanese Dogwood (Cornus kousa)

This dogwood is the Chinese-Japanese version of our own beloved native species, and a comparison of the two shows that each has much to recommend it. The kousa dogwood will make a spreading tree some 20 feet high in its native land, but generally doesn't get nearly so tall here in the States.

Our native dogwood blooms in spring, while kousa is at its showy best in late spring or early summer. The flowers are borne over a long period of time and are a creamy white in color, often fading to a clear soft pink. It is worth while to grow both species together to prolong the blooming season of this lovely flowering shrub.

The petals of the blossoms of kousa are narrowed and pointed, whereas those of our native species are rounded and notched. The leaves are smaller and not quite as coarse as those of the American species. They are, however, less brilliant in autumn, turning brownish-purple, rather that yellow and red.

The fruits of kousa are also different. Instead of being individual red berries, they are fleshy, pinkish-red "heads," somewhat

Japanese Dogwood

resembling strawberries in appearance. They usually ripen in August.

If you are using kousa in the home landscape, remember that there are subtle differences in appearance according to the angle it is seen from. Its beauty is shown off to better advantage if it is looked down upon rather than up to.

Dogwoods may be planted in either spring or fall and may be increased by cuttings of hardwood taken in October or November. Another easy method is by layering; the trees do this naturally when their branches touch the ground.

Little pruning is needed beyond shaping the trees occasionally, or cutting out suckers to prevent the spread of the bushes beyond their allotted area.

Lilac (Syringa)

Lilacs have come a long way and, while the older single varieties still have much to recommend them, I am inclined to cast my vote for the newer, smaller hybrids which seem far better suited to the small home landscape. These are just as fragrant as the older varieties, come in a number of luscious colors, bear double blossoms, and bloom over a longer period of time. Though they will grow 8 to 10 feet tall at maturity, judicious pruning can keep them within bounds. If you select "own root" shrubs, your lilacs will be long-lived plants and there will be no wild

Lilac

sucker growth from the understock.

A minor objection to lilacs is the unsightly seed capsules, particularly noticeable in the double-flowered types. If you find these bothersome, clip them off with a long-handled tree-trimming tool.

Lilacs are useful as either specimen plants or, planted 5 feet apart, they will make a dramatically beautiful flowering hedge. These hybrids now come in double red, white, purple, blue and magenta. Grow them in single color masses for the most striking effect.

The Persian lilac is, in my opinion, the best of the older lilacs and it is singularly beautiful when in flower. Its slender branches form a shapely bush and it grows about 4 to 5 feet tall. Its flowers, borne in small, sweetly scented clusters, are lavender or white.

Mock Orange (Philadelphus)

I am less fond of mock oranges than other flowering shrubs. They are undeniably fragrant, and their white flowers are attractive. However, after the blooming period is over, the foliage is not particularly beautiful, and they are somewhat ungainly during the winter months when their leaves have fallen.

To many, their exquisite fragrance is reason enough to plant them. If you want them for this reason, choose the smaller varieties which range in height from 4 to 7 feet. There are also dwarfs that grow less than 4 feet tall and some lovely double-flowered varieties which may find a place in the landscape of larger home grounds. The aureus variety has golden leaves, the color being at its best in spring.

Ease of culture may also be considered a recommendation, for all mock oranges may be transplanted bare-rooted in the spring. These shrubs thrive in full sun, but will adapt to light shade. Any garden soil will do for them, but they must be given adequate moisture.

Since blossoming occurs on the branches of

Mountain Laurel

the previous year's growth, pruning should take place immediately after flowering, so a good supply of vigorous flowering wood may be produced during the summer growing period.

Mock oranges are useful for naturalizing. The smaller ones may be used in the foreground of the border, the taller types in the background. Branches of mock oranges provide ample material for cutting and they do a wonderful job of perfuming the rooms in which they are placed. If you have ample growing space, you may decide to grow a few for this purpose alone.

Mountain Laurel (Kalmia latifolia)

The best known and most attractive of the kalmias is the mountain laurel. This native of eastern North America may grow as tall as 20 feet under ideal conditions but usually forms a shrub 6 to 10 feet high.

When not in flower, mountain laurel bears some resemblence to rhododendron with its leathery, 3- to 5-inch leaves. The blush-pink flowers are saucer shaped, often an inch across, and are borne in clusters in late spring. Some of the dwarf varieties have flowers of deeper pink; others have dense clusters of a vivid rose-red.

All the kalmias are hardy, leaf-losing shrubs, and do best in acid or lime-free loamy soil. If you would grow them successfully, dig in plenty of peat moss or compost previous to planting.

Plant mountain laurel in fall or spring, October and April being considered the best months. The roots are apt to be thin and fibrous, so pack the soil firmly about them.

Pruning is seldom necessary and is usually done only for the purpose of training back long shoots to maintain the bush in a more shapely form. Older bushes which have become misshapen may be cut back to the ground, and they will renew themselves by sending up new shoots from the base of the plant. Any necessary pruning should be done after the flowering season.

The best means of increasing mountain laurel is through seeds sown in early spring. Place them in shallow flats or pots of sandy, peaty soil in a cool greenhouse and keep moist.

Propagation may be accomplished by cuttings, layering or grafting. Layering is an easy way to increase your stock. Lay down a low-growing branch, make a slit in the stem just beneath a joint and about 12 inches from the tip. Bury the cut section 2 or 3 inches below the soil and keep moist. When roots have formed, cut from parent plant and remove to new location.

Pearl Bush (Exochorda)

The pearl bush is valued for the short panicles of large, white flowers borne in early June. The pretty green leaves are just developing at this time, so the flowers are prominently displayed.

This shrub will require a little patience on your part, as in its early stages of growth it may tend to be somewhat untidy and rather leggy in appearance. It will, however, overcome this disadvantage as it matures,

Pearl Bush

forming a tall, erect shrub of broad-oval form, 12 feet or more tall.

Pearl bush is excellent for use as ground material, and because of its erect growth it is attractive even during the winter months when the leaves have fallen.

Pruning should be done following the flowering period. Cut out any weak or crowded branches and shape the bush to a sturdy, more desirable form.

These shrubs are accommodating and will thrive in most good garden soils, preferably enriched with an occasional top dressing of decomposed manure or good compost. Plant them in open spots where they will receive full sun.

Three- to five-inch cuttings of young shoots will root readily if placed in a propagating frame during July or August. Or seeds may be sown under glass as soon as they have ripened. It is sometimes possible to detach suckers from older plants in late fall.

Photinia

Photinia, which may grow as tall as 15 feet, is very desirable as a specimen plant and will show off to best advantage if permitted ample space and uncrowded development.

Because of the fine, rather thin twigging, it presents a desirable outline even in winter and has much to recommend it for all seasons of the year. Clusters of ¼-inch flowers are produced in early spring. These are followed by small, brilliant red berries.

The leaves, similar in size and shape to pear leaves, are of a good green color but not glossy and may in some species be somewhat hairy. The leaves usually turn yellow in autumn and, in some areas, may develop a reddish-orange color. This adds greatly to their beauty at this season, enhancing the clustered fruits which remain on the bush for a long time. Sprays of photinia are excellent for cutting.

Leaf-losing photinias are genarally hardy in the North, but the evergreen types will live outdoors over winter only in climates that are relatively mild. Well-drained, ordinary garden soil is suitable, and spring planting is preferable. Firm the soil well about the roots and soak with water. Plant in a sunny location. Little pruning is necessary other than shortening any extra-long shoots in spring.

Privet (Ligustrum)

Most of us think privet is synonymous with hedge, and it's rather a shame that this excellent shrub has been "type cast," for some varieties are beautiful enough to be grown as specimen plants.

If given plenty of space to develop, privet will form a handsome bush. It suffers from crowding and hard pruning. Pruning, when it becomes necessary, should be done after the flowers have faded. I am glad that the fad for shaping privet into globes, cubes or animals has passed. Fortunately, we seldom see this in modern landscapes.

Used as a hedge, privet must be kept within bounds by regular trimming. As a hedge plant it is unquestionably king of the mountain. However, consider using it for untrimmed screens or in a group planting where the handsome leaves will show up to good advantage. Though trimming is necessary, privet also makes neat, easily kept foundation plantings.

Privets have small spikes of white or creamy-white flowers which are very dainty in appearance. The only disadvantage is a disagreeable odor in some species, though not in all. The flowers are followed by large, quite decorative clusters of blue-black berries which birds adore.

All privets are easily transplanted and accommodate themselves to average garden soils. They may be planted in spring or fall.

You may increase your stock by sowing seeds, but since cuttings are so easily rooted this is a more practical method of propagation. Take cuttings 3 to 4 inches long in summer and plant in a coldframe. Keep shaded and moist until roots have formed.

Pussy Willow (Salix)

Few early spring plants are more charming than pussy willows, especially the newer kinds like French pink. Huge, fuzzy catkins of silvery gray turn gradually to a silvery pink then to a deeper rose pink peppered with hundreds of golden stamens, and finally become solid gold. Pussy willow is highly prized for indoor bouquets—and with good reason. For early indoor bloom, cut branches and place them in a container of water in a sunny, warm window around the middle of January. Children have a lot of fun watching the catkins develop.

One of the best types of this engaging little shrub grows about 5 feet tall and eventually broadens out to become the "Mr. Five by Five" of the plant world. This rounded, symmetrical bush has numerous slender twigs with narrow, pointed gray-green leaves.

Pussy willow, like most willows, prefers a wet soil, but will grow reasonably well even in light, sandy soil provided it is not allowed to completely dry out.

This willow has many uses. It may be used as a specimen plant or in the foreground of shrubbery. A pair, used on either side of a doorway will add a bit of magic in spring. Or use them as a low-growing hedge, clipping them to shape when necessary.

Pussy willows are easily propagated by cuttings of ripened wood, the usual length being 9 to 12 inches. Plant these in nursery rows or where the new plant is to grow in the future. Keep the soil moist until roots have formed.

Rhododendron

Let's get something settled right off—all azaleas are classed as rhododendrons, but all rhododendrons are not azaleas. Botanists now include azaleas in the genus Rhododendron, but gardeners still regard these as quite distinct from other kinds of rhododendrons and retain for them their older names.

Rhododendrons come in a surprising number of forms and variations. Some grow into trees; others are small bushes or low, prostrate shrubs. Some rhododendrons are suitable for rock gardens, some are even epiphytes (non-parasitic plants which grow on other plants, deriving their moisture chiefly from the air).

There are also many different kinds of flowers and foliage. Some produce leaves as long as 24 inches, others have tiny leaves barely an inch long. In flower, some are tubular, others are saucer-like, and still others are nearly flat.

Rhododendrons are plants of enchanting beauty but, like azaleas, the limiting factor in growing them is climate. They thrive best in a moist, temperate climate where the heat of the sun is often tempered by cloudy skies, such as the Pacific Northwest. They are of easy culture along seaboard strips, but they are not recommended for amateur gardeners in the central portion of North America. However, there are "mini-climates" in every section of the country, and I have seen rhododendrons growing and doing reasonably well in areas where the textbooks said they would not prosper. If their beauty bedazzles you and you want to try growing them, put them in a sheltered location where they will not be exposed to sweeping winds.

Some garden varieties of rhododendron will thrive in full sun, provided they have sufficient moisture, but shade is better, especially if you live in an area where the summer sun is intense. In the case of the large-leaved kinds, it is very necessary. The leaves will burn if exposed to too much light. If possible, naturalize your plants in a woodland. If your home grounds make this impossible, plant them on the north of buildings, or even the northwest or western exposure. A southern location is definitely not satisfactory.

Remember that exposure to strong light in winter is even more harmful than in summer, for it is then that serious scorching of the leaves occurs.

Soil for rhododendrons must contain an abundance of organic matter. Remember they dislike lime and will not thrive in soil where it is present in any quantity. If necessary, have a soil test made to determine the soil acidity before you plant. If lime is present, dig out the soil and replace it with soil that is acid or neutral. The addition of rotted compost or well-decayed manure will help, along with acid peat moss.

Rhododendrons are shallow-rooted, so the surface of the ground should not be cultivated, as digging among the roots will harm them. Mulch well to keep down weeds, using leaves, peat moss, pine needles, or even sawdust.

Water well, when the weather turns dry. Water thoroughly, at least once a week, especially in late summer and fall in regions where rainfall is not abundant at this time.

Fertilizing is not necessary as long as the

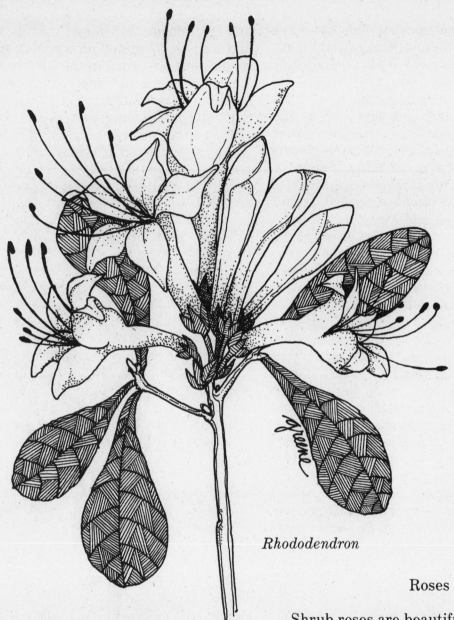

Rhododendron

plants maintain good growth, but as they grow older and use up the nutrients of the soil, it is a good idea to add some well-decayed manure or one of the complete fertilizers recommended for acid-soil plants.

Prune only as necessary to maintain plants of well-balanced growth. Remove all old flower heads promptly before seeds form.

In many areas some winter protection is desirable. Do not use tight-fitting barrels or boxes—the plants do not need warmth but require shade and good air circulation.

Roses

Shrub roses are beautiful in flower, foliage and fruit. They belong to a large family of species of wild types from many parts of the world. From them have been developed many of the roses, such as the hybrid teas, which beautify our gardens today.

Some of our loveliest roses are the result of hybridization, but others have developed spontaneously as "sports." This is true of the moss roses and cabbage roses, which first appeared on plants of centifolia roses. The cabbage rose is thought to have come from the Orient. It grows 3 to 5 feet in height and the soft, pink blooms are very fragrant. Moss roses get their name from the fine, moss-like growth which covers buds, leaves and stems. Many of the moss roses are also delightfully fragrant.

Father Hugo's rose is a Chinese rose which forms a large bush, 8 or 9 feet tall. It has gracefully arching branches and pale yellow, 2-inch blossoms which are delicately lovely even in the bud stage. The fine foliage is bright green, and the blossoms are followed by small, bright red hips and reddish stems, making the bush attractive all summer long.

Plant Father Hugo's rose in an open location. It is useful in lawn beds, in the shrub border and for naturalizing in the open woodland. Prune and thin immediately after flowering to maintain shapeliness.

This rose is readily raised from seed, or additional plants may be grown from suckers.

Rosa rugosa is better known and more widely planted today than ever before. The reason for this popularity is the high vitamin C content of its large red fruits. This rose bears single, rose-red flowers with golden centers which many consider very attractive. The bright green foliage of early spring darkens to a richer green in summer and turns yellow in the fall.

Rosa rugosa is useful for rose hedges and will grow in poor soil. It is very hardy wherever grown and will even withstand salt spray in coast gardens.

Rose Acacia (Robinia hispida)

Rose acacia is the "old country" name for the locust, or moss locust, a shrub of the eastern United States that produces numerous suckers. It is a low, shrubby locust with small rose-colored flowers which appear in spring. The flowers are scentless.

Rose acacia forms wide drifts, due to the suckering roots. It is interesting to note that this plant, which grows from 4 to 6 feet high, has come to rely on suckering to reproduce itself and has almost stopped producing seed pods.

This shrub is very useful in large, naturalistic plantings. It is pretty enough for a border in the home landscape, but impractical because of the difficulty of keeping it in bounds.

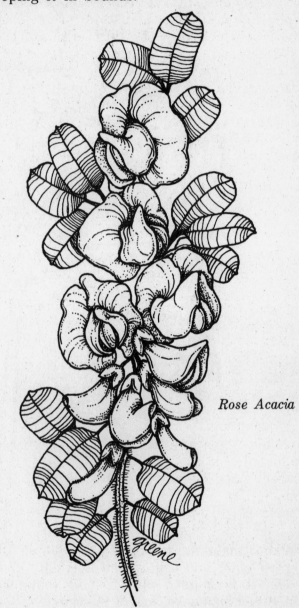

Rose Acacia

Sapphireberry (Symplocos paniculata)

If you would have something both beautiful and unusual, sapphireberry is for you. This rather tall shrub, which occasionally attains a height of 20 feet or more, is well worth planting. It fits nicely into the background of a border and is dramatically outstanding when used as a solitary specimen. In late spring it bears an abundance of fuzzy white flowers which are small but very fragrant. But the pretty flowers are only a preview of the enchantment to come, for they are followed by heavy clusters of beautiful berries which are a bright, turquoise blue. These berries, unfortunately, are favorites of birds, so if you want to enjoy the sight for any length of time, you must find some means of protection. If you don't, they will strip the bushes of their fruits soon after they ripen.

Sapphireberries are also easy to transplant and thrive in any good garden soil.

Skimmia

This low-growing, evergreen shrub which comes to us from Japan has many features to recommend it for use in the landscape. It belongs to the rue family, and the name is derived from the Japanese "skimmi," which means beautiful fruit. The fruit is, of course, its most outstanding accomplishment, but the white, fragrant flowers are also very attractive. There are several varieties of skimmia, all more or less dwarf, averaging between 3 to 5 feet tall.

You must know your skimmias, for male and female flowers are often produced on different plants and it is necessary to grow bushes of both sexes together to insure fruiting.

The best method of propagation is by cuttings, though seeds will grow readily. The reason for propagating from cuttings is that you will be able to grow just the number of plants of either sex that you need, the right proportion being 5 or 6 females to 1 male.

All the skimmias do well in open places or in partial shade. They like a moist, but well-drained soil. They require little or no pruning as they grow naturally into shapely bushes.

Skimmias are not reliably hardy in the North, but will grow in sheltered locations if given some winter protection.

Smoke Tree (Cotinus)

When I was young, I greatly admired a gorgeous smoke tree growing in the garden of a friend. I decided I must possess one for myself. An unscrupulous nursery sold me Cotinus americanus, and the amount of smoke produced by this species is exceedingly small—so check closely when you buy, for the right kind is well worth having but the other, in my opinion, merely takes up room.

The European smoke tree will grow into a large bush, 12 feet high with bluish-green, wedge-shaped leaves. Beginning in June and on through the summer, the bush is enveloped in a mist of silky, mauve-purple clusters of flowers and fruit. These feathery plumes give the smoke-like effect for which the tree is named. Once you behold a mature tree in its full glory, you will not rest until you have one of your very own.

But this wealth of dainty blossoms is not all the smoke tree has to offer, for in autumn the foliage takes on striking tints of yellow, orange and golden red. Add to this the fact that these trees are easily grown in any good garden soil, even succeeding in land that is dry and rocky. As you may have guessed, they prefer a sunny, well-drained location.

Snowball (Viburnum)

To my way of thinking, the fragrant snowball is the most attractive member of the snowball family. To enjoy it most, plant it near your doorway or outdoor living area where its fragrance and outstanding beauty will be prominently displayed. Each May this lovely bursts into gorgeous blooms, covering itself from top to bottom with sachet-sweet balls of delicate pink, which gradually turn a waxy-white. They are so spicily fragrant that you can smell them several feet away, and the dense heads measure 2 to 3 inches across. This shrub also produces bluish-black berries in early summer. In the fall, the leaves turn a lovely wine red.

Spicebush (Lindera)

Spicebush is a large, aromatic, native shrub of the eastern United States, where it grows in moist soil, sometimes making a small tree, 6 to 12 feet high.

The small, yellow flowers, borne in April, are bunched on the naked branches in great profusion, lighting up the hillsides in a shimmer of yellow-green. The leaves, bright-green, oval and slightly pointed, are about 4 inches long and gradually appear as the blossoms fall. There is a good display in autumn of scarlet berries, about half an inch in diameter, but they do not remain on the bush very long before falling.

Spicebush has greater value in the larger landscape than in the smaller home grounds where, in my opinion, it takes up too much room for the rather brief decorative effect it achieves.

If you like the spicy odor, have sufficient room, and wish to grow it, spicebush presents few problems. It should be transplanted with a ball of earth, but will flourish in any good garden soil. Give it a sunny or slightly shaded location. You may plant it successfully in either fall or spring.

Spiraea

Spiraea

The spiraeas are a large family, well known, loved and respected. The name itself refers to the very flexible, graceful branches which were at one time twisted into garlands. This free-flowering shrub is found wild in many parts of the world, including North America, Asia, and Europe.

Bridal wreath, a Korean native, is widely grown in American gardens and is one of the most attractive, spring-blooming kinds. The double-flowered variety is named plena. In both species, the pure white flowers grow in numerous clusters along stems of the previous year's growth.

S. Vanhouttei is a hybrid type which is very vigorous, growing about 6 feet high with long, arching branches bearing clusters of white flowers in June. It is excellent for an informal hedge. S. Henry also bears great clusters of white flowers, exceedingly dainty, and grows 6 to 9 feet tall. S. Douglasii, native to the Pacific coast, is another beauty which grows to an average of 8 feet and bears flowers of a deep rose-red color. S. Billiardii, another hybrid, grows 5 to 6 feet high and bears abundant bright pink flowers in July and August.

You may plant the shrubby spiraeas in either fall or spring, grouping them in the open or in semi-shaded locations.

Pruning methods for spiraeas differ according to species. The double bridal wreath has a rather untidy manner of growth, being rather loose and floppy in appearance. This should be corrected by severe pruning following the flowering season.

Spiraeas which flower from the buds should

be pruned just after flowering by thinning out the older shoots only. Types which flower on the ends of the current year's wood should be cut to within a few buds of the base of the flowering shoots in spring.

All the spiraeas are easily increased by inserting cuttings, 4 to 5 inches long, in a coldframe in early summer. They will even root readily outdoors if placed in good soil in a shady location and kept moist.

Stewartia

Stewartia is a beautiful shrub which may reach the noble height of 50 feet when grown as a tree. Most, however, are grown in shrub form and pruned back to 10 feet or less.

While generally considered a bit large for the shrub border, stewartia is very desirable as an individual specimen.

Mountain stewartia bears handsome white, cup-shaped flowers from June through

Stewartia

August. These are often 3 inches across and are crowned with golden anthers. The foliage is very colorful in autumn, changing to golden-orange and finally to scarlet.

Showy stewartia, preferred by many, has dramatically beautiful purple stamens. This variety, however, does not rival the brilliant autumn color of mountain stewartia, for it assumes a rather drab, purplish look as fall approaches.

Stewartias are well worth growing, but remember they must have considerable space and need a sheltered spot and moist, well-drained soil. They are easily propagated by layering a few of the lowest branches in late summer. Cuttings are slow to take root, but seeds may be sown in a slightly heated greenhouse in spring.

Summersweet (Clethra alnifolia)

Clethra alnifolia, sometimes called the sweet pepper-bush, is native to the Atlantic coastal region and is the best and hardiest type for general cultivation. It prefers low, moist, open woodlands where it grows 5 to 9 feet tall. Easily established, this shrub produces suckers freely and will soon form a large clump. It is fine for naturalizing in large plantings, and specimen plants are charming even for the smaller grounds.

The fragrant white flowers are produced in dense spikes during a long season. These occur on the upper portions of the upright branches in erect, cylindrical clusters at a time when few other shrubs are in bloom. The pointed, rather oval leaves, about 3 inches long, turn a clear light yellow in the fall.

Pruning should be done as soon as the flowers have fallen. The oldest branches should be cut down to the ground, and the oldest parts of other branches which have flowered should be removed. Vigorous young shoots should be allowed to grow to provide blooms for the next season.

Clethras are surface-rooting shrubs and benefit greatly from a good mulch placed on the soil in early summer. This keeps the ground cool and moist, providing them with conditions similar to their natural environment. They will grow in open locations, but prefer light shade.

The leaf-losing types may be planted in fall or spring, but the evergreen ones are not hardy and are suitable only for mild sections.

Clethras may be increased by cuttings, but lifting the freely produced suckers is an easier and more popular method.

Tamarix

Tamarix is a slender, delicately beautiful tree or shrub whose special attraction is its tiny, ethereal pink flowers. In most kinds, these occur on the upper part of the stems, creating a very showy effect.

The leaves, which add greatly to the dainty effect, are very tiny and in most species a grayish-green. They are borne on very slender branchlets, many of which fall in autumn with the leaves.

Tamarix, while they will thrive in inland gardens, are best suited for coastal areas where they are very resistant to sea air. Where they can be successfully grown, these shrubs are useful for hedges, either informal or clipped. They will thrive in either light or heavy soil and will even grow in sea sand. Best suited for mild climates, they may be grown in colder areas. Even if they freeze back during the winter, the roots seldom freeze and new shoots will spring up.

Tamarix may be increased by cuttings, generally made 9 to 12 inches long and inserted in a coldframe in summer or fall.

Tree Peony (Paeonia)

If this is not the loveliest plant ever to bloom in a garden, it is at least equal to any other. The beautiful, fully double, goblet-shaped flowers often measure 8 inches wide. Their rich-hued petals have the soft gleam and translucence of Oriental silk. They bloom lavishly, sometimes producing as many as two hundred blossoms on one tree. The blossoms may be pink, silvery white, golden yellow or deep crimson.

A further point in favor of the tree peony is their dwarf size. They seldom grow taller than 4 feet, making them suitable for the small home grounds as well as the larger landscape.

The tree peony is a leaf-losing shrub with either single or fully double blossoms. It thrives in ordinary garden soil, but will give forth more blossoms and grow more vigorously if this is enriched with leaf mold and, if clayey, some sand.

Try to choose a location which is sheltered from the east. These shrubs, which begin active growth while the frost is still on the ground, are unlikely to be damaged by severe cold in winter. The young shoots are, however, liable to damage by late frosts unless in a sheltered place.

Vitex (Chaste Tree)

The attractive heads of small lilac or white flowers borne by the chaste tree from late June on through the summer are its chief contribution. The chaste tree may be either leaf-losing or evergreen, and though they may be killed back to the ground in the North, they will still bloom the following summer on the current season's growth.

This shrub may grow as tall as 10 to 12 feet, but can be pruned back much lower. The leaves are interesting, being divided into 5 to 7 leaflets, gray beneath and dark green above. Chaste trees will thrive in any reasonably good soil, but they do like a well-drained location and full sun.

Transplanting should be handled with care. Preserve as many of the roots as possible, being careful also to see that they are never exposed to sun and wind. Spring is the best season for transplanting. Keep the plant moist until well established.

Weigela

Weigelas are well-formed shrubs, growing 4 to 5 feet tall, which will grow and thrive just about any place. They are deciduous and of erect growth, and are valued for their handsome flowers borne in great profusion in late spring. They are moderately hardy but may be killed back. If your winters are very severe, plant weigelas in a protected area or give them some type of protection.

Weigelas like full sun but will grow in partial shade, though they will not bloom as abundantly. A good garden soil, neither too wet nor excessively dry, will accommodate them very well. Occasionally some compost or well-decayed stable manure may be dug into the soil. If you have clay soil, lighten it with sand and organic matter.

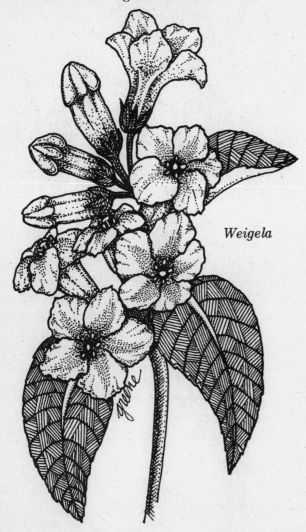

Weigela

Since weigelas produce their blossoms on shoots of the previous year, pruning should not be done until after the flowers have faded, cutting out any crowded older branches.

Since weigelas produce their blossoms on shoots of the previous year, pruning should not be done until after the flowers have faded. Cut out any crowded older branches and remove any weak or badly placed stems. Weigelas make vigorous growth, so pruning is very necessary from time to time to admit light and air and to give the bush a more attractive shape.

The blossoms may be white, pink, deep rose or crimson, with many variations in between. Some are pink with yellow in their throats. The individual blossoms are rather small, but they are borne in such abundance that they more than make up for their size.

Weigelas are easily increased by making cuttings of half-ripe wood and inserting them in a coldframe in late summer.

Winter Hazel (Corylopsis)

The graceful, dainty winter hazels are an especially welcome sight in early spring when we have grown weary of winter white. The pale yellow, delicately fragrant flowers are borne in pendant catkins before the appearance of the foliage, and their great profusion makes up for their rather small size.

The best known varieties of these shrubs come to us from Japan. Of these, spike winter hazel grows 3 to 4 feet tall, and the drooping catkin-like clusters are often 2 to 3 inches long.

Winter hazels are leaf-losing shrubs, several of which are hardy in sheltered locations even as far north as New York. Others should be grown mostly in mild climates. They prefer a sunny location and will thrive in a light, well-drained soil to which a little peat has been added. Place them where they will be sheltered from cold winds, and give them a good mulch in the autumn.

You may increase your stock by sowing ripe seeds in pots or flats of sandy soil in a cool greenhouse or coldframe. Cuttings of half-ripe or partially woody shoots may also be rooted in a propagating case. Keep the frame closed, adding moisture as needed, until the roots are well formed. A third method of increase is layering.

Witch-Hazel (Hamamelis)

I've always found the witch-hazel truly fascinating. This shrub or small tree may grow as tall as 20 feet. The bark and leaves are used to make a soothing lotion. It grows in woods of the the eastern United States and Canada and, left to its own sweet will, its jointed, curving branches twist and point in all directions. The forked twigs have been used for divining rods, adding further to the plant's mystique. In fact, the name "witch-hazel" refers to this use.

Unlike most of the shrubs we have discussed which bear their flowers in early spring before the leaves appear, witch-hazel does just the opposite. After the leaves die, in October or November, the witch-hazel puts forth its blossoms. And a sight to see they are, for they grow in dainty, feathery clusters. The fruits do not ripen until the next year. Then, in what seems to be a final burst of mischief, the seeds shoot from their small, woody capsules to a distance of several feet!

The most decorative witch-hazel is the Chinese one. It forms a spreading bush or small tree which may eventually grow 18 to 20 feet tall. The leaves are larger than those of other types, being 3 to 5 inches long and 2 to 3 inches wide. It bears very fragrant, golden yellow flowers, which look a lot like primroses.

If you can obtain seeds, you should plant them and then be patient for they often lie dormant for 2 years before germination takes place. Cuttings are difficult to root, but occasionally you may be successful in layering branches in the spring.

Plant your witch-hazel in well-drained, loamy soil, mixing in some compost and peat. Choose a sheltered location with a southern exposure. If you want a truly dramatic display, plant it where it will show up best—against a dark background. The flowers are not injured by light frosts, and the wood is seldom damaged by cold.

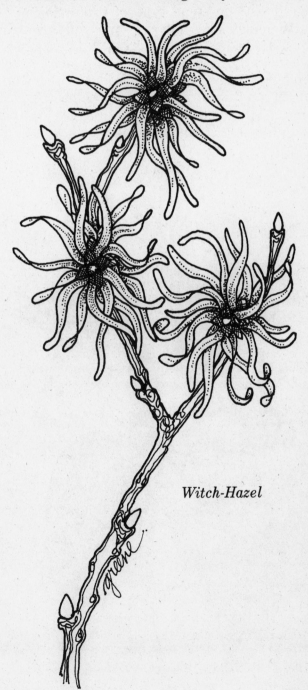

Witch-Hazel

ADD THESE OUTSTANDING BOOKS
TO YOUR GARDEN LIBRARY
AT ONLY $1.95 EACH

America's Master Gardener, Jerry Baker, shows you how to have the garden of your dreams. Easy-to-follow directions and large, clear pictures make these the perfect books for beginners as well as experienced gardeners. Each book in the series covers a different garden subject and each one is chock-full of facts and the know-how to help you make friends with your garden.

IN THIS SERIES

Make Friends with Your Lawn—21558
Basic advice on lawn care, including mowing, watering, fertilizing, and weed and pest control. The book also contains plans for building a new lawn and for rebuilding an old lawn.

Make Friends with Your Annuals—21559
How to select annuals for specific purposes, how to grow from seed, and how to cultivate and protect. The book includes an invaluable list of annuals with descriptions, illustrations and cultural requirements.

Make Friends with Your Evergreens and Ground Covers—21560
How to choose evergreens for beauty and economy, and how to plant, feed and care for them. Basic information on landscaping or re-landscaping.

Make Friends with Your Fruit Trees—21561
Fruit trees to provide shade, natural fences, or patio decoration. Good cultural practices and pruning advice. There is detailed information on the most popular fruits and on nuts, grapes and berries.

Make Friends with Your Vegetable Garden—21562
Where to place the garden, how to make a garden plan, tools and equipment needed, and everything else you'll need to know for the vegetable garden of your dreams. A special section on how to grow and dry herbs.

Make Friends with Your Roses—21563
How to choose the right roses for your garden. Also included is detailed information on soil preparation, setting the plants, cultivating, pruning and propagating new plants.

Make Friends with Your Flowering Shrubs—21652
A fact-filled guide to choosing and caring for these beautiful shrubs. Features a special list showing height at maturity, geographical zone, and other vital information.

Make Friends with Your Perennials and Biennials—21653
This useful guide tells how to naturalize perennials in meadows, shady spots and marshy areas, and how to plan and care for a perennial garden. An unusual section on biennials offers hard-to-find advice on these two-year favorites.

Make Friends with Your House Plants—21654
A complete guide to indoor gardening, including facts about soil, pots and potting, fertilizer, watering, and propagating. A section on decorating with plants adds valuable pointers for showing plants off to their best effect.

Make Friends with Your Shade Trees—21655
A valuable guide to selecting the right trees for your yard and budget. The book includes advice on landscaping, planting, feeding, and general tree care.

Make Friends with Your Flowering Trees—21656
A wealth of information on landscaping, good planting practices and tree care. Features a list to help you pick your trees according to color, size and shape.

Make Friends with Your Bulbs—21657
A detailed guide to choosing the right bulbs for your garden, for every season and location.

Mail this no-risk form today

To Your Bookseller or

Simon and Schuster, Publishers — Dept. BR
630 Fifth Avenue
New York, N.Y. 10020

Please send me the book(s) checked. I enclose payment with the understanding that any book(s) may be returned within one month for full refund.

Name_____

Address_____

City_____State_____Zip_____

$_____ENCLOSED.

Please check books wanted—at $1.95 each
- ☐ MAKE FRIENDS WITH YOUR LAWN—21558
- ☐ MAKE FRIENDS WITH YOUR ANNUALS—21559
- ☐ MAKE FRIENDS WITH YOUR EVERGREENS AND GROUND COVERS—21560
- ☐ MAKE FRIENDS WITH YOUR FRUIT TREES—21561
- ☐ MAKE FRIENDS WITH YOUR VEGETABLE GARDEN—21562
- ☐ MAKE FRIENDS WITH YOUR ROSES—21563
- ☐ MAKE FRIENDS WITH YOUR FLOWERING SHRUBS—21652
- ☐ MAKE FRIENDS WITH YOUR PERENNIALS AND BIENNIALS—21653
- ☐ MAKE FRIENDS WITH YOUR HOUSE PLANTS—21654
- ☐ MAKE FRIENDS WITH YOUR SHADE TREES—21655
- ☐ MAKE FRIENDS WITH YOUR FLOWERING TREES—21656
- ☐ MAKE FRIENDS WITH YOUR BULBS—21657